BY JOSEPHINE W. JOHNSON

SEVEN HOUSES

A Memoir of Time and Places

JOSEPHINE W. JOHNSON

WITH ILLUSTRATIONS BY PETER PARNALL

SIMON AND SCHUSTER · NEW YORK

For Grant

I

"OAKLAND"
KIRKWOOD, MISSOURI

1 At midnight, in the darkness of New Year's Eve, I struck a match and lit a candle. A candle of many colors, rose and purple, sun-yellow and blue, made by a child. Colors of such beautiful translucence that a rainbow seemed burning in the room. It was dark in the kitchen, a cave sheltering the candlelight. Outside in the cold night there were gunshots,

celebrating the new year, the sound of a siren, and then silence.

After midnight it is morning, but the darkness goes on and on. All through the darkness I have a vision of people's minds as lights. Some like long lighthouse beams, some fire-sparklers the summer children swing, there are bonfire lights flaring up in unexpected places, or the warning lights on cars; urgent lights in doctors' intercoms, or minds whose lights are sputtering fuses, frantic and going out. And some are like blinking traffic lights, yellow and caution, or others mysterious lanterns moving through the woods, appearing and disappearing, moving steadily down stream banks to dark caves. Some minds move weak and wavering like candle flames in the wind, and some are globes of pure light, steadfast and warm, great harbor lights, but rare, O rare.

The rainbow candle burns an upward steady flame. No wind in this room, this house, this morning of another year.

In the silence, the marvelous, deep, candlelit silence of this sheltering home, one's own human life seems extraordinary, a small wick, burning and burning in a house of bone. And under one's feet the world, this planet with its rooms of fire, burning and burning in a house of stone.

At this hour, years ago, my mother waited for the morning of her marriage. Rituals and symbols of newness and everlasting change, that were, for her, of wrenching newness and beginning. To leave "Oakland." One did not leave this family home lightly. One never left it.

When I last saw this home, this place in Kirkwood, Missouri, that made and molded my mother and for that reason is part of me, it looked very cold and severe in the snow. Cold red brick and white-rimmed windows. Wicker furniture on the porch. A wicker rocking chair with snow blown under it is a chilly sight. Children coasted down the hill and skated on the pond. The stone pillars are still at the gate, but the granite Neptune was gone. Every soul that ever lived there is gone.

Mother's memories were parceled out to us in precise sentences, gentle comparisons or wry descriptions. The little remembrance she wrote for us three years before she died was reticent. Perhaps she recognized in our request, as in all too many things, the condescension and rejection of my generation for the past, for the people of that past and the way of life that was Oakland. The gardens and the gatherings, the visitors and servants, the beautiful horses and the summer afternoons in the hammocks. I am sorry that I never told her how profoundly moved I have been for many years by this place, this house and the family, which, without romanticism, had such a strain of dignity and grace, of thoughtfulness and intellect. As children, with all that innocent cold cruelty of children we listened raptly to the tales of Oakland, and then gloated over whatever little failings, idiosyncracies, small evidences of mortality we could discover, dropping unconsciously from the lips of authority. From those elders who held us in submission but could not persuade us of their divinity.

The house was not beautiful. It was huge and red brick mounted on white stone. Thin squared pillars held up the long encircling porch and there was a square tower room with a delicate crown of lightning rods like lace. In pictures it appears cold, rectangular, severe, each window with square white eyebrows. More like the seminary for young ladies which it finally became than a home so full of life and memories that I who never lived there am sometimes sick with nostalgia, as though invisible roots pulled back across space and years. Actual pain, that seems at times absurdly more in the stomach than the heart or mind.

The house stood on a slope above a large pond—a pond with a huge granite figure of Neptune at one end with a gray stone beard and a trident imported from the World's Fair in St. Louis. I have an odd cantankerous yearning after statues. For the great iron St. Bernard that guarded Seven Gables in Kirkwood. Even sundials and birdbaths affect me. Children should have something to touch, rub their fingers between great gritty toes. Climb on the backs of iron dogs with iron curls. Stare up into impassive marble faces that do not suddenly swivel around in rage and ask what are you staring at. Don't poke. Don't point. Hush up. Great marble folds of drapery that never move. Wide laps for sitting.

Mother too seemed invulnerable in her coolness, but it was a very thin envelope, holding together a lifetime of emotions, will thwarted and will fulfilled, prejudices and ideals—ah! it was the ideals, the standards, that dominated! The standards that were possible to maintain as long as one was willing to sacrifice other tenants of the body. And as long as one had private means to maintain life, and such moral and social standards as were somehow set by Oakland and by a life lived largely among other women. There were six girls and one boy. And female relatives and friends who visited in waves or came to live.

Oakland was ten acres of great oak trees. They shaded the stern house and the driveway that curved up from one street and went out another. There were flower gardens, vegetable gardens, an orchard and a bowling green, stables and servants' quarters. It was not grand. It was not mysterious and regal, nor was it opulent. It represented a great deal of money, won by a great deal of work (and the absence of income tax) at a time when such things were possible of achievement by an immigrant child from Ireland indentured as a servant.

What do I know of my Grandfather Joseph Franklin? He was a legend and a hero to his family of girls. He was a great and good man, a family man, Papa, a radiant loving father and husband, a witty man, a serious man, a man who loved people, entertainments, conversation, sports. An acute businessman, a man who made a modest fortune to hand down to all his daughters and his one son. A man who had ethics, honor, prosperity—and grief.

He was born in March in 1836 in County Cork, Ireland, and of those years there is a little scrap of paper called "Recollections" which begins "Reasons for writing":

Since departure of my dear one, I have been going

over the past, and find how little I can remember and how pleasant it is to recall old memories, and so I think that for my dear children's sake I will try and bring back as much of my life as I can and note it down for their future profit and pleasure.

The first recollection of my childhood days is of a storm. May my last be brighter. One morning coming downstairs at the old house where I was born I remember a bright fire in the grate, and looking out the window, I saw the effect of the storm, and that which dwells most in my memory was seeing the slates strewn about the yard. It must have been a famous gale, for I can remember the clergyman preaching on it the next Sunday and comparing some people to the rush that went before the blast and thus escaping, while others were like the sturdy oak, firm and proud—and prostrated by the rushing wind.

That terrible scourge, the Irish fever, visited our home and a young brother and sister were taken. I shall never forget the cold feeling I had when taken to see them after death. Every member of the family but myself and sister Mary was taken down at this time and after their recovery both she and I were attacked, but lightly. I remember having to wash dishes and make myself useful about the house as no one would come near the place.

Like most people of his time he lived in the constant presence of death—the young died, and the old did not linger on in sterile sleep as now. But he chose to live more fully in this constant presence.

The young man who, according to the story, walked down from Alton to St. Louis on the ice, as the river was completely frozen in that year, signed what seems now a strangely poetical, yellowing paper, indenturing himself

to the service of William Fitzgibbon, General Merchant,
to

learn the department of his Art and Business called the
General Trade, and with him after the manner of an
Apprentice, to dwell and serve, from the day of the date
here of unto the full end of four years and eight months
. . . during which term the said Apprentice, his said
Master shall faithfully serve, his Secrets keep, his lawful
commands everywhere gladly do; he shall do no damage
to his said Master, or any of his goods or chattels, nor see
it done by others, but that he, to the best of his power
shall forthwith give warning to his said Master of the
same, he shall not waste the goods of his said Master, nor
give nor lend them to any; he shall not commit fornica-
tion, nor contract matrimony within the said term. Hurt
to his said Master, he himself shall not do, . . . he shall
not haunt taverns, ale houses, nor play houses, not absent
himself from his said Master's service day or night un-
lawfully but in all things as honest and faithful apprentice he shall behave towards his said Master all his
family, clerks and servants during the said term of four
years and eight months.

And then in return for this the said William Fitzgibbon promised to

teach and instruct with due correction, finding unto his
said Apprentice, during the said term . . . meat, drink
and lodging befitting such an apprentice AND it is also
understood that the said Joseph Franklin shall contribute
the sum of one pound 5 shillings for levy allowed the
privilege of becoming a member of the House Library
and 2/6 shillings as a subscription to the Medical Fund

of the Establishment. In Witness thereof the said William Fitzgibbon has set hand and seal this day of October in the year of our Lord, One thousand eight hundred and 48.

The Kirkwood railway station was at the gateway. Morning and afternoon and evening trains ran hourly throughout these years. "Came home on the 2:10," Aunt Florence wrote. ". . . Went in on the 10:15—Papa home on the 5:15." Special trains were arranged for the Literary Club. This sane and sensible form of transportation brought my own father at six-fifteen each evening and he walked three blocks home under the maple trees winter and summer, spring and fall, as did all the Kirkwood husbands scattered out along tree-lined sidewalks and wearing straw or bowler hats according to the seasons. No one was really better in those days—but the days were better. Nostalgia is deep inside me for the days themselves, for the land that went with each house, each family, the gardens, the trees, the evening sounds—and silences.

Grandfather Franklin, arriving on the five-fifteen, walked up his curving driveway and into a hall that was the size of public reception rooms today and opened out onto rooms on every side, sitting rooms, dining rooms, smoking rooms, and staircases ascending. Its walls had a peculiar wrinkled texture that simulated something and was painted gold. It resembled a great gathering of lizard skins, and even the huge potted plants, the swags of Christmas smilax cannot quite cover it. There is much dark shiny leather furniture. Much dark shiny wood. And dark shiny figurines with bronze drapery and the mantelpiece beside the mirror, and in the mirror is reflected Joseph Franklin's portrait from another room. Lace curtains hang in the windows. Bowl-shaped shades cover the lamps. It is, by all our standards, very disorganized—even homely. But it is interesting. It has texture. (Nobody knows that better than the maid or daughter whose turn it is to dust all those tortured little bobbins that fret the rocking chairs.)

Though it is a strange medley of plaster, glass, leather, wood, horsehair, felt, plush, lace bronze, wool and linen, it is not in flux. Each piece has a history, a place. Each piece is a favorite chair, a gift, a souvenir, a product of the household—Alices, Joes, Marys, Robbies . . .

The little split-wood chair was sitting outside in the rain when Mother and Aunt Alice came to visit one time. "What a shame!" I heard Aunt Alice whisper. "It used to be in the upstairs nursery at Oakland."

"Oh, never mind, Alice," Mother said.

"But it's survived so long!" Aunt Alice said. "It ought to be treated better."

And then Mother said a few words wearily that I've carried like seven old men of the sea ever since. "Oh, Alice," she said, *what difference does it make anymore!*

The library at Oakland stretched from floor to ceiling, wall to wall. You can see a glimpse of the bookshelves from the hall. What were those books? Endless debates between science and religion, Darwin's *Origin of Species*. Browning's poems—lots of limp leather Brownings in small volumes. (Have you read Browning lately?

The man's extraordinary. Full of dark horrendous scenes and tortures. I wonder what those ladies of the Browning Clubs were really up to.)

Walk on over the leaf-patterned carpet, under the gas lamps, and there is *Pickwick and Sam Weller* in a huge gilt frame. It hangs above the piano. This is a busy room. There is a "dado" of landscapes near the ceiling. And pictures of landscapes on either side of the great Pickwick. I have a recent yearning for pictorial pictures again. To stand and look far back to distant mountains, to which tiny boats are heading, and on the shore tiny people picnic, while near at hand a family group of peasants—or of wealthy sightseers—gesticulate, smiling or sad, dangling long ribboned hats, patting long-haired, carefully painted dogs. The storytelling picture, the romantic painting—but at least doing something. Not blobs of color.

There are tall vases on the mantel, a shiny black bust of Beethoven on the piano. The chairs have carved legs, flowered seats, curved rockers; antlers sprout from the walls; flowers sprout from flowered vases. The Mexican vase is there. The bookcases have glass doors. Parlors, hallways, living rooms all seem to flow every which way, kept in order by massive sliding doors with square carved panels. There is so much going on in silence!

All the Franklin aunts are in the earliest of the pictures. It would seem to be a dark day. In November perhaps. The trees behind the firs are bare. There is a little house with a churchlike window. Grandfather bearded and capped is the very middle. But there are many people I do not know. Men in bowlers and high-top hats, and a strange greyhound under Aunt Edith's hand. Aunt Alice is there, hatless, with that sweet aura of childlike innocence which lasted her eighty years, but the curls— and she was the only Franklin that had naturally curly hair—the curls are pulled back by a ribbon. And Aunt Mary looks plump and young—maybe for the last time in her life, because her beloved sister Florrie is still there, and there is Aunt Laura, solemn and waxlike, hair skinned back, Laura who was to live forever, outlasting every sister, and Aunt Edith in a white crocheted shawl and Mother in her tam o'shanter, long plaid skirt and high button shoes. Good Lord, the clothes! They fascinate and appall. They fit so close it is hard to breathe just looking at them! They are curiously beautiful, and the little Franklin faces of the girls rise up and out of them like pale buds emerging from wrapped and rewrapped stems. Take Edith's dress. A plaid wool, waist tight as a sheath, arms, bosoms, waists, hips, plastered with heavy material as one builds a figure of wet papier-mâché or burlap. And over this two velvet lapels, and a velvet bow at the neck and her lovely face drowned with heavy braids of hair as her mother wore it. Those dresses must have been quilted with minute stitches, those handmade dresses of boned, ruched, gored, fluted, seamed, overlaid, tucked, hemmed, scalloped, smocked, laced and lined material, which was heavy to start with.

Clothes shaped women's lives. It shapes children's minds and hearts through all the ages. I know that. Children should not be forced to wear clothes they hate. There is no wretchedness to compare with the child who hates what he or she is wearing.

The horror of the black tights, for instance. Far from the lovely ballerina tights today. They were footless and footloose. The name was a misnomer. They rode up the legs and drooped in the seat. They showed through the stocking. The perpetually wrinkled stocking was bad enough in its natural drooping state, but to have visible beneath it the dark shadow of the tight! No protection from the rain or cold of nature could compensate for this grim storm inside the stout and discontented child.

The men are caped and muffled and carrying walking sticks. There is something impressive about those heavy capes. A powerful and masculine emanation. Who is the tall man in a stovepipe hat with great white side-whiskers but no beard? This shrubbery is infinitely becoming on either side of piercing eyes. And there are unknown Other People in tartans and hats with plumes, and children in long velvet coats to the ground.

One's emotions upon discovering unknown children of unknown people in a family album have never been very creditable. Who are those creepy kids? What are they doing there? The boys' stockings are always more sagging, their faces longer, the girls' hair is more naturally curly (but one does not concede this), than that of any relative or known friend of a relative. It does no good that we have been told a dozen times, "This is May," or Lily, or Libby Aberstacht, "she was a good friend of your Aunt Mary's. That's Normy Biegel, a sweet bright boy, who came out with Will's friend to go bowling . . ." In a month they are forgotten. "Who's that?" And privately to oneself, "What a bore." They ought not to be there at all. Albums are for the Family. It took somehow the burning glass of attention away from oneself—who, of course, was not there at all—and intimates a wider life in which one never would have played a part. And one detects a certain edge of impatience at the obvious lack of interest which caused us to forget this Normy Biegel who was a sweet bright boy. Oh he was, was he? He looks like a halfwit to me. And his eyes are squinchy.

Sometimes one forgets they were alive outside the pictures, that they were people of flesh and blood and faults and passions. Even the diaries, the notebooks, the letter, which bound them together and kept the record, have a restrained and far-off sound. "How cold and stiff this book will seem," Aunt Florence wrote in her diary New Year's Eve. "Who will think what a burning heart I had when I wrote it."

She kept a journal of the year 1883, when Oakland was built and the family came out from St. Louis to live there, a year full of life and sickness and death. She did not know that her own mother would die a year later. "We had callers yesterday," January 2, 1883, begins. "Not very many for we've not received for several years, and so our friends were rather out of the way of coming. However we had over fifty." . . .

Sunday, Jan. 7
    Of course none of us went to church today for we have four wards, and it takes all our efforts to keep the patients comfortable and quiet. Laura has diphtheria.

Jan. 8
    All better today, thank God. Little did I think when Mamie gave me the book how soon it would record so

much of sickness and misery. But O yes I think I can say "Thy will be done."

Jan. 12

The patients still all convalescent. . . . I feel very gay and lightheaded to think we have been spared so much of what might have been.

Jan. 18

Robby has pleurisy. Maury Peirson died. Mamie still miserable but able to be dressed and laid on the sofa.

Jan. 22

I wish I could make myself interesting to the children. Class of nine dwindled down to two. But perhaps it's the weather. Yes I'd like to put it down to the weather. . . . Poor Didge quite hoky. J. took a plunge into a puddle and has diphtheria.

Jan. 27

Papa brought home the plans. O dear how much things cost! I wonder if we will be able to bear the expense. Mr. Barr approves the country place. Mr. Reed has heard of our plans. A jolly row. [Mr. Barr of Famous-Barr. Mr. Reed the family friend and minister.]

Jan. 28

Joe sick.

February 2

Alice joined hospital. If Toots only keeps well now.

Feb. 4

Papa went with other jurors up to Jefferson City to get a high license put on whiskey shops.

Feb. 6

Little Jean Cochran died this morning of diphtheria.

Feb. 7

Doctor sick. Water frozen.

Feb. 9

Bought plum-colored cashmere. Mrs. M. recommended seamstress.

Feb. 10

Mamie half up and around. All the children can come to meals.

Saturday February 17

Just to think our house will cost over $12,000! Isn't it frightful to contemplate such an enormous price . . . also all the outhouses to be repaired.

Feb. 18

First time this year I've been to church. It seemed good to be back again. Mr. Reed's sermon was a real nice one on "The Love of Christ constraineth us."

Feb. 20

Yesterday Mama and I called on Mrs. Shaw and then Mrs. Morrison (who was out), Mrs. Chancellor, and Mrs. Porteous (out too).

Feb. 22

Papa has brought home the plans and specifications. *I hope he will be as pleased with the reality as with the pictures.*

Feb. 28

L. C. has failed. Utterly and entirely. Swamped the whole family. Poor Aunt Mary. Papa loses nothing, but

O dear I wish we had never introduced him to the land directors. Two months so full of trouble!

Jan. 29

Ma and Pa nearly done up. Aunt Susan an awful cold. Mary not so well. Edie better than usual. Josie doing as well as can be expected. George in bed—sore throat. Alice and Ethel doing pretty well considering. Bertha nearly ready to give up with rheumatism. I'm so stiff I can hardly walk.

Jan. 31

Mama signed deed to Oakland property.

Sept. 3

This is moving day. Mary and Annie took the five children and part of the live-stock. Bertha to follow on the 3:24.

Mother went to look for a pig. . . . I helped put down carpets all morning.

Oct. 8

Ethel's birthday. It is also the third anniversary of our horrible burning. [Florence and Grandmother Franklin were burned by an explosion from a leaking gas fixture.]

December 31, 1883

Well how strange it is to think that it is really a whole year since Mary presented me with this book! The last day of the old year. Am I sorry? Glad? Sad? I do not know. Indifferent most likely, for though it is an undeniable fact I can hardly appreciate it. It has been such a pleasant year in so many ways and such a sad sad one in others. It began in sickness the very day after New

Year's day and we had nearly a two month siege—rheumatism, pneumonia, diphtheria, chills etc. O that is a hard time to remember. Yet we had much fun and excitement during those weary days. Father then conceived his brilliant plan of moving to the country,—where we are, though this night a year ago no-one would have dreamed of it even! Yes, during all the sickness we had much fun over the planning of our mansion. . . . But saddest this year was the death of dear little Thaddeus. O that was awful. And O so many others are gone. . . . Perhaps in a few years I may carelessly turn over the leaves of this till then sealed book, and see here and there a brief short notice. How cold and stiff it will seem. Who will think of what a burning heart I had when I wrote it. . . . When Mary gave me this book I thought to myself surely not enough will happen to fill up even these small spaces, but often I had to crowd out events not having room to record them. . . . Surely on the eve of another 365 days I need not sigh and say I *hope* something will happen. Something has happened. Something will always happen. But now Good-day Old Year. . . .

Oakland, home of the Franklins in Kirkwood, Missouri

Above, Grandmother Jane Ann Franklin

Opposite top, Grandfather Joseph Franklin

Opposite bottom, Joseph Franklin with four of his daughters, Edith, Alice, Laura, and Ethel

Opposite top, Living room at Oakland, with picture of Pickwick and Sam Weller, landscapes, and piano

Opposite bottom, "The furniture was big and solid, shiny and carved."

Below, Entrance hall at Oakland hung with garlands for Christmas

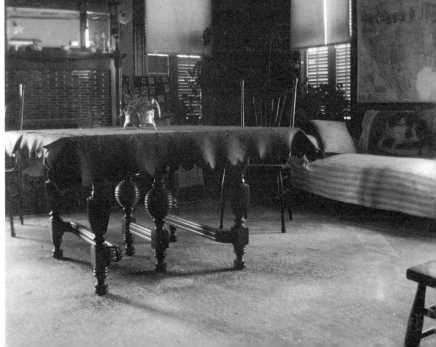

Franklin family and friends at Oakland. Grandfather, bearded and capped, in the middle.

II

CHILDHOOD HOUSES

2   I have lived in many houses, many places. The
first houses, the childhood homes, formed and
channeled the flow of childhood life inside
them. When I look back I think of all these places, these
homes, as shelters on a long slow traveling. A long
journey from Oakland to the Old House, that first house
of my own. Some houses were shelters, much loved,
through which one flowed as the gemmules flow through

the parent sponge, and some as close as the shells of tur-
tles, protection, enclosure, shells as much a part of oneself as the head and claws.

The second house, called simply and starkly by its
street number, 203, brings an odd first recollection to my
mind. The scratchy dryness of paint peeling on sun-
blistered wood. Dry hot paint on white porch railings.
On green shutters. To climb on the porch railings was an
adventure. To look down on the spirea bushes foaming
white below. To push someone off the railing was the
same as pushing them over Niagara Falls.

And after the scratch of paint I think of steps, of
steps and stairs. Number 203 was a small house, but
steps and stairs were everywhere.

We sat on steps a lot. Sat there convalescing from
mumps. Dreary, slowly deflating children. Kinship to
the frog receding. A miserable ridiculous disease, each of
us more absurd-looking than the other.

We sat morosely on the back steps in the cold, in
the sun, waiting to be allowed inside after a certain quota
of fresh air was absorbed. I liked steps. One could use up
all sorts of space. Adjust one's legs, sprawl up and down.
Kick people cautiously. (I remember childhood now as
years and years of slow-burning fuses which never quite
reached the dynamite. I had savage daydreams. Have
them still.)

Steps were everywhere. Front-porch steps, up which
old ladies climbed on the arms of their grown sons; steep
indoor steps with railings polished by hands, down which
we never slid. Backstairs steps, back-porch steps small
and utilitarian, scary wood steps down into the cellar

from the inside, concrete steps up to get outside the cellar, steps down into the darkness of the fruit cellar under its earth mound and its little chimney. (And only a jar of pale white peaches on its shelves.) One house reached a cresendo of steps, back, front, attic, barn, porches, and even the walk descended to the driveway with steps.

Steps are orderly, and yet they have scope. They go up. They give a view. They make a child taller. You can run sidewise dangerously. You can inflict harm on the one on the step below you if you choose. They make splendid seating arrangements for family portraits. The second row is best to hide one's fat legs and drooping "tights." It sets one apart from the chubby, still-happy three-year-olds who smile, stare and stick their tongues out at the camera.

In the big drafty hall we tried over and over to climb the gold stair ramp made by sun motes in the morning. If one believed hard enough, if one ran fast enough, it would be possible. It seemed *important* to do this. It fascinated us endlessly. I even pretended I had done it once and had risen above Gravity, that uninvited godmother at my birth. The squat oleacious figure, wrapped in heavy cotton stuff in lieu of gold christening robes. Black cotton folds and big sensible shoes. The uninvited who brought her offering in a cardboard box instead of a silver casket. And smelled of oakum and wet muskrat. Gravity. Gravity. The mysterious polarizing power of magnetic rock within the earth. Here is my gift, she said, to this odd child, born June, 1910. Born within the margin of the Gemini's power and doomed already to a dual soul. What more appropriate gift than this huge and invisible load of gravity? A big slow child, and her father will call her "old slow" with mock endearingness and all her life will be an interesting and blind and back-breaking struggle against this lethargic substance which I bring. A blend of seaweed, tar and wet mosquito netting. Deep water and deep snow. Infallible!

In 1910 the world of war had not reached into every pore and crevice of life. On the day I was born, according to the New York *Tribune*, a man left his anvil at his father's blacksmith shop long enough to get married and immediately returned to resume operations with hammer and anvil. His bride went home alone. Theodore Roosevelt wrote a letter to President Taft. "Men who saw Taft at the White House came away and in strictest confidence told the secret to others. So it became known all over town. At the White House all that could be learned was that such a letter had been received. . . ." Magistrate O'Reilly was angered that a man was brought before him for selling ice on Sunday. . . . Theodore Roosevelt went to church and the Reverend Percy Olton preached the sermon.

"A new age is at hand," he said, "the age of brotherhood, and it has its problems. The greatest problem of all perhaps is to bring the corporate conscience up to the level of the individual conscience. Men who as individuals are honorable and above reproach, are, in their corporate relationships, almost entirely without any Christian standard of ethics. . . . The trusts and labor unions have come to stay, and both will bring the greatest benefit to the greatest numbers. The grave peril is that corporate conscience which is being evolved as a result, will be inferior to the individual conscience." All eyes were turned on Mr. Roosevelt as the clergyman spoke of the trusts, but he gave no sign, and sat immovable. . . .

June's "birth gem" is an agate. A deeply disappointing stone to a romantic child. I searched slyly among other lists of birthstones, hoping the *Idyls of the Months*, by Mary Fathbury, could be found fallible. Once on another list I found the pearl. But the sapphires and the diamonds belong to April, and none of us four girls was born in April. May got the emerald and July the ruby and not a one of us was born in those months either. And we decided by the book.

The important things of childhood have very little to do with reality. Sometimes it is an absurd world of precious stones and lovely *Idyl* ladies with absurd enormous eyes. This gray-bound book with the title in faded gilt, letters like soft fainting eels, and a great gilt fairy with a silver crescent moon was the dream book of our childhood.

Each month had the picture of a lady and a poem and a birthstone. "Look," I'd say. "My hair is longer and curlier than yours. *I've* got all those beautiful roses!"

"You've got the agate, though. Agates are dumb. You're dumb like an agate."

"I don't care. Anyway you're just silly. Look at those pigeons coming in your house!"

"Those're doves, not pigeons."

"You'll catch cold standing in front of the window in winter. You're stupid."

And so on and on. It took me a long time to laugh at

myself—either real or imagined. It took almost thirty years, in fact. (It wasn't that I didn't find things funny —but not myself. O solemn sacred sober citadel. Laugh at that? Never! The whole thing being held together with flour paste would have crumbled.) And the *Idyls* were written in sweetened flour paste.

> June with health and wealth and many happy years
> Wears an agate lest her sunshine turn to tears.

The odd sullen agate is not a distinct mineral species; agate means a group of amorphous and cryptocrystalline forms of silica. The stone is chalcedony, variegated, arranged in stripes or bands or blended in clouds, or showing mosslike forms. It is found in ancient lavas—filling the cavities produced by the liberation of gases as the molten rock cooled down.

I disliked everything about it—its muddy ferrous color, its "amorphous, cryptocrystalline" forms! But how appropriate a birthstone it has proved to be for one who is continuously a cloudy mass of the dead and the living, the trivial and the great, the near and the far, the faint and the strong, the immediate and the distant. In whose kitchen the breakfast dishes mingle with thoughts of the dying in Vietnam, ghosts, pain—men in prison peer at the innocent blackboard with lists for the living. Bread. Soda crackers. Call Jane. . . .

I wanted the sapphire. There was something wholly feminine about the sapphire. Something rich and regal and romantic. Where did I ever see one? My vision came from colored pictures in the dictionary and from my own imagination which created something great and glittering, sky-blue and shatteringly beautiful, and probably of glass.

But what a beautiful June maiden was mine to make up for the agate! With long curly hair to the waist, a little red beret, a red tunic held by a gold cord and a green skirt to the ankles—no, to the tip of the bronze booties. And a huge platter of roses held in smooth extended and rounded arms. A mean little mouth, dropping scalloped eyelids—but the curls, those long waving chunks of hair! Believe me, I lived in this watercolor image! She gave me prestige and glamour. She was, in the mysterious mysticism of childhood, the real me.

I did not know then the meaning of the Gemini and the Crab above the poems—my birthday, the twentieth, being on the borderline between the beginning and the end of these astrological signs.

This searching into the past follows a trail that can only be described as lurching. A path made by the feet of wrenched instincts. Which is the normal lot of children.

But I have no intention of describing the long subterranean world of childhood. The contemplation of the vicious and the vulgar that went on under the round ribbon-topped skull. The child that contemplates the outer world from behind green glass veined in brown (agate eyes, in fact) and then turns inward to its cave of murder and grotesque and routine torture from which it emerges fresh and innocent and vulnerable as though the bones of parents, friends and siblings were no more than seashells in this cave. These caves are known. They are not washed clean by time. They have been explored and overcharted, but they hold some power still and we leave them alone to walk in the no less mysterious outer world where people spoke above our heads of a God above their heads; and trees, sun, mantelpieces, upper bookshelves and lights were all above and out of reach.

Truth, which one defines as a collection of facts, a report of what was really said, done or happened, took quite a beating in that fog-shrouded world of communication between adults and children. On the wet gray beaches, through the wet gray veils, we heard a tremendous sound of roaring, of crashing and receding. "What was *that*? What was that terrible sound?" "Never mind—you'll find out someday." . . .

The slimy and cretaceous life that lived in the sand, the eyes that popped and sank . . . "What was that? . . . And that?" "There was nothing there. Go outdoors . . . go indoors. Never mind. Go back to sleep." . . . Under our feet only the wet gritty sand was real. The million thousand particles of glass that repel each other. It could not be hidden, because it stuck between the fat toes. And besides, they did not want to hide it. Sand makes pearls.

Sometimes great ribs sailed in on the breaking sound. Or vast dying whales were stranded. You have to explain a dying whale. "He is very sick. You must be quiet and patient." "Phew, what an awful smell!" "Go outside. Never speak that way again!" The guest room door was closed. The fog swirled around and over the huge shape. Only the odor of the dying was still there.

In the year before I was born the family sat to be photographed on the front porch. Each person clearly him or herself. Aware of their role in life. Their *place.* There were places then.

Grandmother Johnson, serene to smugness, white-shirted, high-necked, long-sleeved, hands in lap. Aunt Elizabeth beside her, hands not so serene, still a little gay. Her place beside Grandmother for all the years of Harriet Johnson's life, until the hour of the satin-lined coffin (at which time she looked much as twenty years before, pink-cheeked on the white pillow, under glass). Her shirtwaist was frilly with lace, rimless glasses, a little smile above the pincushion chin we inherited. And Dad above on the left, derby on his head, mustache and glasses, hand casually on his knee, a gesture unusually serene, paternalistic, happy to have his family, his relatives all grouped around him. And Mother in a white shawl holding Mary Lib, with her tiny chipmunk face. In the exact center upper level, Miss Sallie Stevens, enormous, white-haired, leaning back in the chair to breathe above her corsets, presiding like a huge monolithic God-figure, a female Buddha fully clothed, and this time without one of her extraordinary hats.

Before I knew her back in the red-mahogany photographs when old and minute Mrs. Stevens was still alive and Miss Sallie still had a waist, she wore a bonnet-shaped hat with black plumes; and the black plumes come to 621—Miss Sallie under a creation with a huge rhinestone buckle holding back the plumes that must have once been an entire ostrich.

But the years of the plumes did not compare to that great navy-blue-silk-ribbons year. A whole sink schooner afloat on the white foam of her hair (or a floating island of those water hyacinths that break off and barge downstream).

My father did not have as many relatives as my mother. Miss Sallie came with Mother. The large package deal of marriage. We did not like her, which was not her fault. We were afraid of her deep voice and her piety and her size. Our antagonism was a cross to Mother, who had real affection for her, at least a recognition of her merits and some sense of duty born of old ties and old affections, and old habit. When she came to dinner I imagined myself inside a private telephone booth at my own place. I shrunk to invisibility and ate my food encapsulated in this booth.

I tried not hear her telling for the hundredth time (three times equals a hundred in those days) of her friendship with dear Reverend Philip Brookes. That sainted man. His name is forever confused with a picture of a stream babbling between blue forget-me-nots. But at all events when one does not like a person their presence seems to thereby swell and fill up the whole house. One *knows* they are there even were one not hushed when they were sleeping. "How long is she going to stay?" we asked. First boldly and bluntly and then with increasing sullenness and timidity—and in whispers.

When Miss Sallie was not with us we went to visit her in a boardinghouse. The feeling that children had, when visiting, of being on sufferance! (And not suffer the little ones to come unto me, either.) The prim cold eyes of the landlady, the nervous "Don't touch" of Mother. We squirmed, tiptoed across the room. Peered fearfully at the parrot. Ran back to our allotted chairs. Waited. Waited. Endured. (Ridiculous to remember the waiting more than anything. To remember the discipline more than the love, to remember the quality of breakfasts—the lumpy cream of wheat, the sour oranges . . .) Where Miss Sallie boarded there was this parrot, and a stained-glass window on the stair. Not a picture-telling window—just colored glass. That was good for five minutes. How clearly the torture returns. The waiting. The boredom. . . . Well, I've finally learned that a little means a lot. Each day of the dying is as important as the years and years of their lives—as *our* lives. . . .

I think of warm summer nights in Bowling Green with Dad's relatives. Of those long dull evenings of mosquitoes and palm-leaf fans, stars and night moths. Those vast stretches of time which passed, somehow, in conversation—conversation which I suspect now had no more value than if we had sat immobilized before a Big Blue T.V. Eye. . . . "How many gallons of gas did you use on the drive up?" Long silences. Recipes. . . . We did not hear lovely gory stories of hospital, local scandals, religious discussions, old talks—I do not remember much of anything but weather, past, future and present weather, travel conditions and the heat of those upstairs rooms. We found private solace in the brick paths of Aunt Elizabeth's garden. Her tiny jammed-up garden in rich black soil, her dank dark chicken yard, the outhouse and the beautiful blue delphiniums and the lilies. There was an apple tree, and a few fallen apples. A tiny garage which held her little car, jacked up all winter. The grass seemed always scorched and thin and the garden damp. We had so little patience with old people then! (Were they really very old?) We noted all their mortality and held them responsible for it. Their warts and long ears, liver spots and then cramped hands. Their deafness and impatience and obtuseness. "Now Jo is going to look just like Cousin Pearl" (and Cousin Pearl was enormous as a hippopotamus). What immortality did they achieve by "seeing" Cousin Pearl's weight, Aunt Kate's eyes and Uncle B.'s eyes (Uncle B. who sat and chewed tobacco in a corner and never said a word) in each of our amorphous and reluctant faces? . . . We gave them no credit for anything, for their lives which had been lived. We were told very little about their lives.

Relatives are not Other People. Other People had some strange ownership of sophistication and romance. Other People had huge begonias and pipe racks, grown sons, late hours, and went to picture shows.

We had ferns but not begonias like Other People. Sisters, not brothers. Children hold harsh court and judgment against their elders. What did the begonia-owning children hold against *their* parents? The absence of the Johnsons' horse or hyacinths or something of no merit to us because it was always there and known?

We had a few Rose of Sharon bushes with their dingy purple-pink flowers. Varicose-vein color. But big, and a bush that bloomed big flowers was exotic in spite of everyone else having Rose of Sharon. I believe they were held in awe and respect because of their name. The Bible was really a sacred book in my childhood. "*Never* put another book on top of the Bible," Miss Sallie said.

Want to feel wicked and daring, children? Pile a couple of schoolbooks on top of that black grainy cover. We did. We giggled and snickered, and then took them off and felt bad. I still feel a vague cold premonition when I do it. Even without intention.

Meal memories swirl through all the other houses and places of life, like odors and smoke, coiling and linking habitations, but of the eight years of meals (three times 365 times eight) which I must have had in that house I remember nothing, absolutely nothing, except the April Fool muffins of bran, and wanting to sprinkle sugar on my lettuce and leaving the room in tears because it was not allowed. For a person who has always thought a great deal about food this is very odd. I remember the bell one could push under the table which rang in the kitchen behind the swinging door. I remember the wounded cat wrapped up in clean rags and convalescing in a box over the heat register. I remember ferns on high stands in the window. But I do not remember a single meal on the table. But from that dining room the people in *books* rose up and left for their walnuts and wine . . . Sherlock Holmes . . . Henry James . . . and all the events of Alcott's paper lives, more real than my own, took place in this house, and Beth died in the bedroom upstairs—the one to the right of the stairwell, with its western view of the barn lot and the stable. And the coffin of that poor neglected mother in the Irish folk tale bumped up those stairs to find the bad Irish daughter.

The bedrooms had slanting ceilings and I remember peering through narrow bars of a bed. I think those sliding sides may well have been used long past their appropriate time.

How stiff and slow the memories come. Something is wrong. Like children arriving in starched clothes to some function they would rather not attend. I see the red ring on Dad's forehead from his stiff straw hat. I hated those red rings. I see bookcases with glass doors and smell the brown chemical smell of Argyrol. One can never forget it. Huge rags covered with the stuff from the dripping of our noses. Surrounded with the brown rags—like cars in a garage being oiled and greased. Miles of torn-up rags. We looked and felt disgusting. The common cold was the ruler of our childhood. Winter a miserable season for every man, woman and child. The white iron bars at the foot of the bedsteads was the winter view. Fevers and phlegm the climate.

It has been observed, and rightly, that Mother would rather have had us sick than well. It simplified a harried life. She knew where we were. She had us under control. Well, I don't blame her anymore. I stopped blaming her for all that went wrong. The planter cannot help plant the seed that cannot help growing. If there seems a safety in sickness now, if the Nirvana of convalescence is a substitute for the Everest of achievement, she could not help it. We have had plenty of time on our own to change things around, and, as neurotic adolescents, we scorned personal safety and dealt so savagely with sickness and recovery that it is remarkable we are alive today.

I can recall the scent of dahlias, a faint and cool smell. Of sweet alyssum like honey. And hyacinths, the like to which there is nothing in the world. Those crisp waxy petals, the stout lavish body, so firm and full and bourgeois! So utterly romantic, satisfying and fulfilling to the child. Preferably blue, then pink, and lastly white, at that time. Easter and hyacinths. Hyacinths and Easter.

And then dear Miss Mack with her great black Indian braids. Outsize in that small Victorian world. Crammed into a starched nurse's uniform. Starch . . . aprons like something fired in a potter's furnace—a ceramic madness that represented the triumph of Hygeia over life. But then Miss Mack would let down those torrents of black hair and we all dressed in our little limp Indian outfits and blankets and danced—possibly even in bare feet—for five minutes. (What did we think as children about Indians and the national acts of genocide? I do not have the faintest idea. I am ashamed to investigate.) We dug for old Robby the pony's body, poking the earth with a wooden spoon, and found maggots. . . .

Patterns of life were established here. This was the most important time and place of our years. Lifelong burdens assembled and interlocked.

Here I lined things up in parades. Played with dolls. Set scenes where nothing much happened. Planned speeches. Hid. Found spots to be alone. Told a lie or two. Suffered intensely. Mended broken dahlia stalks. Dressed and undressed dolls in a vicarious world of glamour. Waited for the school picnic. Waited for Christmas. Waited to grow up.

Here grew the seeds of deviosity, ingratiating blooms. . . . We were afraid of our father. I learned to woo, to fake, to be silent or to sidle away into books. I became a nice child. An acceptable quiet child. A rather stout slow child. Bomb-shaped, but slow-burning, long-fused. I suppose he loved us all, but I have raked memory over and over to rock bottom and I cannot find one shred of evidence to present here. (See this bit of clay—it was part of an Aegean vase. This gold link—that was once a chain.) Nothing. But he was a good man. He was honest and handsome and—from his letters to Mother—lovable.

The land, though small, had a field at its side, a rough uncut field filled with daisies and Queen Anne's lace and not kept cut, possibly to discourage us from crossing and lingering along the fence line that separated us—and indeed successfully separated us—from a family with boys. I grew up in an atmosphere electric and prickly with distrust of boys. They were not really human beings, I think, in Mother's mind. It was an atmosphere that had its effect, as I suppose a plant that grew in a murky pre-storm season all its life could not fail to show some sign of this strain.

We walked on sidewalks under large trees. We walked to church. We walked to school. Spring beauties grew near the sidewalks. Violets grew along the roads. Roots loom large in my memories. Roots close to the walks. Roots across paths. The infolding of great roots against which children leaned. It seems incredible now.

One night in Kirkwood an old man's shanty house burned down on the street behind us. A huge packing box gone up in flames. We ran and watched. I remember a sound of crying somewhere. Was the old man trapped inside? I don't think so, but it was one of those things hushed over. The border at which the censors stood between childhood and the hooded adulthood. The world of mystery. Everything is told now. The censors and the inspectors and the custom officers are all gone. And that's good. Thank God for that. Except God's gone, too. Childhood is swept away by all the fires since. A man woke at night when a firebomb was hurled into his house by a Klansman and died. A bomb exploded inside a church, children were blinded and killed. Churches— black churches—burned all over the South. Crosses burned. The country of Vietnam burned from one end to the other. A man driven by sorrow and horror burned himself to death on the steps of the Pentagon. And then young men burned little pieces of paper that represent their bondage to the great system of rule by fire, and the outcry of righteous indignation was deafening.

It's a long way from the little hiss of the rockets going off in the summer evening. And the magic stars that the sparkler gave off in the dark. Running and whirling the prickling stars on the lawn in the warm evening air. Dad made queer worms come out of the wood with a match. What were they? These things boiled out slowly, and it happened only on the Fourth of July. There is a little flag on a stick, and Dad has on his stiff straw hat, and we have big hair ribbons on, bare legs, and sandals. And Miss Sallie is sitting in a rocking chair in her shirtwaist and black skirt, and her gold watch pinned on her enormous front. It is a long low table outdoors and we are all completely absorbed. Everything is forgotten but this curious magic happening, the worm and the sulphur smell from the burnt match. And the little table had a burn mark on the wood ever after. This struck me as a sign of unutterable daring, that only an adult could do—perpetrate something that would leave a burn mark on wood forever. Somewhere I had gotten an awesome respect for property, for this was only the little table we used outdoors for making mud pies, and Dad could not get his knees underneath it.

Sometimes I had murderous childhood dreams of everybody else sponged out and myself in command of all the world and its material possessions. What did one *want* as a result of this lonely power? I do not know.

Kirkwood was full of dark library rooms, dark woodwork smelling of pipes. And I keep trying to recapture a sense of safety, of belonging, surrounded with book-laden shelves in a dark room, like a crab forever trying on new shells for one that suits him and satisfies some nameless need. "This is the room," I say to myself, and then quail because it is the room of an elderly clergyman retired . . . or "This is the room" and am embarrassed because it is the replica of a Spanish nobleman's . . . "This is the room," but it always turns out to be also something one cannot bear—age . . . conservatism . . . great wealth . . . reaction . . .

We can no longer afford the luxury of that synthetic grief which doused us as children, that literary sorrow which fell in great spring floods around us, when we were surrounded by the small imaginary suffering creatures found in books; books whose very covers seemed spongy with the grief inside. Grief from a cruel and hostile world, and grief rising from the incontinent sins within. The starving black-clad figure of Sarah Crewe, sharing her bun with the crippled beggar girl, enduring hunger and cold and orphanhood, the sadness of Black Beauty shambling in old age through the London streets, poor Uncle Tom—what tears one shed, hiding in the closet under the staircase, over the memory of his bowed and broken head! And there was the death of Beth in *Little Women*, and the death of the poor frail mother in *Lady Jane*, wandering with her little girl in the heat of New Orleans; and the death of countless brave and beautiful dogs, who seemed more subject to mortality than to life. As I look back over our reading it seems a shambles of women and children left widowed and orphaned (the good brave men died first) and noble dogs stretched out at their feet, and all remembered through a steady fall of childhood tears.

And not only the sorrow that came from cruelty and death, but the tears shed for the nonattainment of the unobtainable, for the impossible goal of sheer perfection. Just in case any child of my generation got the idea that life was enjoyable and beautiful on its own, and that we were here in the pursuit of happiness, *Stepping Heavenward* was there to chill off that one. *Stepping Heavenward* was the long saga of the discipline of a semi-orphaned girl upon whom the author visited the usual viscissitudes of one person's life plus all of those normally spread over the population of a city. Her inability to be all things to everybody as well as God caused her much anguish, and in the end her triumph of perfection struck me as a cold and meager thing. (She was permitted to die slowly of a wasting disease so as to have more time to prepare to meet her Maker.) And the long steep stairs toward heaven had one plump child stuck at the bottom. (But not unscarred, oh, no—left short with permanent uneasiness, if that is any satisfaction to that sadistic lady author who beat the conscience of her little paper heroine from the first step to the final landing, and made her pay in sorrow for every feeble stirring of the self.)

And, finally, there was *Little Jakey*. *Little Jakey* was in a brown book with line engraving illustrations throughout, so that if the written word didn't hit you over the heart, the pictures would. Little Jakey was an orphan ("My muzzer ce die, my fodder he die"), and blind, and with the face of an angel and long golden curls. His muzzer she cry and cry, throughout the book, and fodder was a drunk and he beat ze muzzer, and in the end little Jakey gets a chill from losing his way in the orphanage grounds and lies on the earth all night, and sees his mother and little sister coming down from heaven in long paths of light, and he too dies, and no reader with a mustard grain of sensitivity and the ability to read German dialect will finish the book without he or she cry and cry as little Jakey goes up to heaven.

What this ocean of death-reveling, conscience-beating books did to the generation that wallowed in it, nobody really knows. One child might flourish in the bog, grow water-repellent, buoyant as a lily pad; no tragedy in life taking him unaware, who has survived the paper death of Lady Jane's mother, or Beth's soul winging off at dawn. There are no statistics on who survived the trial by water and who went down, done in by ancient tears, and carried this synthetic sadness, this glorification of unmitigated grief, into a life that might have found better ways of dealing with its own.

3   We went to a private school in Kirkwood for the first few years. A very good school with only one teacher.

There was a swampy place at the edge of Miss Blanche Byars' school. The sidewalk went over a small bridge, in fact, and a stream ran under. Violets grew there, and we were allowed to pick them. Other children always found the biggest violets and picked the most, no matter how greedily I tried.

I pushed a child down the front steps. Was it I or someone else? I'll never know now. Someone was pushed. (A process goes on here. One simply rejects the act done, as not being done by oneself. Or, once admitting the act, no longer believes it evil. There were reasons, good reasons. And, being punished, society, not self, becomes the enemy.)

We wore rubbers in wet weather, and *after* wet weather, and in the possibility *of* wet weather. I remember the feel of dry mud on rubbers, and the thunder of blood in one's head stooping over to pull them on, or flat on the ground pulling and tugging. (They *had* to be tight enough to stay on, they *didn't have* to be long enough to get on easily. One is stuck with the lessons of life as surely and securely as one is stuck inside one's rubbers, with one's name printed inside but gradually fading.)

I remember the squeak of boys' corduroy pants. We envied boys, dreaded them, hated them, admired them. Loved them when they were funny. Today I will willingly sell my soul to anybody who can make me laugh.

Miss Blanche played the piano masterfully. By which I mean she inspired her pupils with the feeling of power over piano. All was under control. Each black or white key responded with sharp distinction. (Her manner of music may well be the reason I cannot bear the sound of piano music today, but at the time it seemed that *this* was mastery and music of the highest order, which I, although a reasonably bright child in everything else, could never emulate. What did she play? What did we sing? "The Star Spangled Banner," and various hymns—"Jesus will comfort me . . ."

I recall distinctly the feeling of floating around the sky on a large puffy quilt, a comforter. The huge eiderdown quilts of incomparable warmth and lightness that Dad brought us. Eventually the infinitesimal feathers began leaking out. One quilt was re-covered in moss green, still huge, warm, comforting as Jesus never was; the other went to Algeria for the refugees. The piano was in the small same room as the desks; when one left the room the outside child squeezed between his desk and the piano. But when the top was closed no child's hand ever touched it.

One went out into the hallway to study. A profound privilege and delight. One child at a time. The small hall's long bench covered with a coyote skin. That was the privilege. To sit on the dry gray hair and fiddle with snarling teeth, the cold glass eyes, the pink painted gums. A faint dusty smell came out of it. Dried wildness. Light over the staircase came from a stained-glass window. Small, no Bible people, just blue and red glass. The stairs led up to Miss Lulu's private rooms where we were forbidden to go, and of course did not. When everything is in scale, and the people and the place and the time go well together, obedience, harmony, flourishes without too much force. One child at a time on the coyote skin in the hallway. No children in the private rooms upstairs. At recess you may go as far as the violet beds. No farther.

It occurs to me that in writing "comforting as Jesus never was" I have said a good deal that I did not know was there. God yes. Jesus no. God the Father, that was whom we feared. Jesus the man was an alien figure. Never really believed in as the legitimate heir. Or, possibly, being a mortal man, never fully understood or felt by a Franklin child. All girls again. But God the Father —that was whom to watch out for.

In the second classroom, where we went when we rose, turned and left to study history and English, there was a small statue of Mercury in plaster marble. Forever poised, fig leaf plastered tight, ridiculous hat on head and wings on feet. On the west wall where the light shone on its glass was a brownish Burne-Jones *Galahad*. A sickly handsome knight in armor, looking faint. My strength it is the strength of ten because my heart is pure.

And then there was the little bell on Miss Blanche's desk. The little bell. Ting! Rise. Ting! Turn. Ting! Leave the room. A forgotten yearning fills me. To get hold of that little silver tinging bell. The power-structure symbol. Not to destroy it. Oh no. But to be the tapper of that little bell. To make others Rise, Turn, Face the aisle—O power incarnate under my fat grubby finger!

Power emanated from her plain person. But we did not hate her, nor did we hate school. Too much was going on. We got so much attention!

We were elevated—levitated—lightly to another plane of life. Blanche Byars' gift, the gift of a born teacher. When she read to us out of *The Voyages of Ulysses*, I listened, I was there. In that boat, on those waves. At the mercy of the great winds. When she stopped we asked her to go on, but she wouldn't. The south wind was for tomorrow's reading. Ulysses tossed on the waves until Tuesday. I have never been in a classroom since where I watched the clock and hoped it would *not* strike the hour.

Somehow I remember everything being in scale. The people, the place, the time, going well together. We never suffered from the usual cruelty of *other* children. We received so much individual attention that the rules were not oppressive. Miss Blanche represented authority in its most pure and pleasant form. Vincent Byars, her father, was a Greek scholar, and he was honored and revered in his own time. There was an intellectual community in Kirkwood, whose vitality was very real. Blanche Byars, our teacher, was the treasured leader, the chariot driver of that vehicle by which we were to journey to a kingdom which she, and all her family, and all my family, valued beyond all material and even spiritual matters—the intellectual kingdom of the mind.

The war was unbelievably remote. Dad dressed in his army hat and puttees and trained once a week with the National Guard. I spent long hours arranging the Schoenhut dolls in patriotic tableaus. The Schoenhut dolls were rare treasures, so jointed that their arms and legs and wrists could move in an almost human fashion. I orated for them, poking flags in their hands (by shoving the hands together, the stiff fingers could be induced to hold the wooden stem of a flag). I remember the speeches. "War is a noble thing. War brings out the great sacrifice in men. . . ." I was only seven. Troop trains went through the Kirkwood station, and once the school was let out to march down and wave to the men.

It is not a very vivid memory. It was hot and the men in khaki seemed to sprout from the windows of the train in an insectlike explosion.

When the war's end came I wrote my first poem. It was inspired by a huge newspaper drawing of Liberty, Justice and Humanity striding along in a blaze of sunlight bearing flags and banners. (It may well have been by Charles Dana Gibson.) The poem follows.

> Out of the light
> Come the conquerers three,
> Liberty, Justice and Humanity.

I had found my niche in life.

4 The next house was large and beautiful. When the aunts built 621 in Kirkwood they saved the oak trees. We played under oak trees a hundred years old. Oaks were first base and third base in our primitive game of baseball played with tennis rackets. It was easier and more fun to use a racket than a bat. And thus began our wanderings from the masculine conventions which imply that only sweat, fury and certain set weapons make the game worthwhile. (And somewhere every now and then a dying man may ask who made the rules of that great monstrous game in which he dies— *for* which he dies.)

(These ghastly faults and shifts which take place internally . . . the geology of the mind and stomach altered without a sound . . . without warning!)

I was no good at even this unorthodox game, but at least it gave me a chance to hit the ball once in a while.

We were heirs to Aunt Laura's garden and to all the bushes—the firebushes, the barberry bushes nine feet high and thorny as hell, the white spirea bushes, silent waterfalls of flowers with a faint and plumlike fragrance. Rosebushes higher than a man with huge flowers whose petals seemed to melt in sweetness, falling along the driveway after rains. Bushes with bird nests in them, bushes to hide under, creep behind. Bushes that were houses and barricades, safety and danger. And there were a few white bridal-wreath bushes. A sparsely flowered bush, but beautiful with its tight bouquets of blossoms, and its mysterious and lovely name. . . . "You'll never be a bride," she said. I believed that. This seemed a part of that peculiar climate in which I lived. The porous soul absorbing all that might destroy its growth, rejecting nourishment while seeking for it desperately. We'll never know. For meantime, in another part of the forest, the world went on preparing changes which, to put it simply, will make good become evil, and evil become good. The roots of the god Random.

The garden, when we came, had a little lily pond,

lined with tiny tadpoles. We came, child barbarians, to a ladies' garden, and we fell into the pond (or were pushed) and Dad put up a high spiked fence with a gate and chain around this tiny pocket of water. It was hideous and inappropriate and typical. A row of ugly iron spears and a chain and overprotection . . . over protection. I see little tadpoles peering through the spears.

Ferns and lilies of the valley grew in a narrow space outlined by the brick paths near the cellar steps. Soft cold red brick with moss growing in the spaces between. Pauline came and went, up and down the cellar stairs. She had a last name, she was Mrs. Smith, but that was not how we ever thought of her. The laundry room was dimly lighted, the stairs inside dark, narrow and dangerous. We were hardly ever allowed down there. For a "liberal" family such as the Franklins were, this absence of light and safety seems very strange. Pauline washed and ironed down there under a naked bulb, and she could see wheels and feet out of the little area windows. She had many children of her own, and all the trials of blackness and poverty. It astonished me to hear from Mother that she came to call years and years later, and spoke of me as an individual, in whom she had had some interest, and made some discerning statements about our childhood. I would have thought she scarcely noticed us, having so many problems of her own. It startled me. Humanity in humans always does.

I do not remember my childhood as a happy one. It was too full of a morbid and passionate sensitivity to both beauty and pain. But it was rich, immeasurably rich in light and shade and texture and color and the thousand faces of nature. Translation: Josephine was a fat child who ate too much, had very little self-confidence because of other children's criticism and bullying, and therefore got a sick stomach from excitement. Took criticism hard and was therefore in a continual state of suppressed anger and feeling of inferiority. Was no good at games or any athletics whatsoever. Had a morbid conscience which she managed to get around by subterfuge almost continuously. Was as anxious to save face as anyone in the Ming dynasty and built up an elaborate and transparent superstructure of hypocrisy, which became as necessary to preserve life as any other vital element (and which, until thirty-five years later, nobody showed her was not really necessary at all).

The arbors grew over, the rose vines sprawled, the wooden seats decayed. The "summerhouse" I remember without much pleasure. There was always the rivalry for the hammock, and the nearness to the cow pasture. The damp grass was full of violets, but one had to watch one's feet. Getting damp feet was a high crime. The cow pasture divided us from a street of thin wooden houses where the Negroes of Kirkwood lived. We never went there. We never even walked by there on our way home from school. Their street was not finished as was our street. It had no sidewalks either. All the streets in Kirkwood ran with mud at first, eventually they became asphalt-covered, but not the ones behind us. You could hardly get a buggy through the ruts. They were rural alleys through all my childhood years. I cannot remember thinking of this as anything unusual, as anything but a fact. One of "our" side streets crossed these alleys, and you could look up the hill and see dogs and chickens wandering about, pots of flowers on porches, and, as from an enormous distance, children of one's own age in shapeless dresses staring back.

Black children went to separate schools. I did not think that was strange, nor that their school was old and shabby. What happened to them when their grammar-school days were over? I did not know, it never occurred to me to even think about it then. One felt sorry for The Poor in General, but I had no idea of the plain stark zero end that was their future in those days.

In Kirkwood there was, at that time, a place for everything, and everything was in its place. The poor, the widows, the Negroes, the children. Each had a place. And they stayed there.

There were hiding places in this house—hundreds of hiding places there. One could flee along halls, duck into closets, pound up the back stairs, down the back hall, through the upstairs front hall under the midnight moon picture Mother painted, down the front stairs, pause on the landing. One's heart in curiously good shape for all the real and vicarious terror it responded faithfully to for so many years. Terror in dreams, terror of teachers, terror of being shamed, being strangled, drowned, smothered, terror of failing, and so on. But the delicious terror of hide-and-seek, of fleeing through hallways, up-stairs and down, the feeling of banisters under one's hand—that was something marvelous and not of the other terrors known.

From Oakland the Butterfly Picture was inherited. A huge collection in a great gilt frame. The frame heavy and carved. The mounting a masterpiece.

In the center of the butterflies and moths from Brazil is a hairy tarantula. The moths are of incredible beauty, the butterflies an iridescent shimmering blue and purple, the beetles make a mosaic of shining emerald shapes, and at the bottom is a huge owl moth with gold-rimmed eyes on its wings. . . . I like this blue one best —no, this one. I like the big green beetle best (we all loved the great Blue One in our hearts). "The spider is still alive. I'm going to open the glass and get him out and drop him down your neck and he will kill you." . . .

All the beauty and terror of the word *jungle* was in that picture. We never tired of looking at it. It was our movies, our television, our terror stories and our visions.

(Who cares now? In that same-size frame, night after night, any child can see all this in motion—spiders and butterflies and tortoises, horses and monkeys and men dying.)

The Butterfly Picture hung at the foot of the stairs. The light from the north window on the landing came down and shone on it. A curious adult dream comes to mind. I am standing at the foot of the stairs facing the Picture, one hand on the round oak newel post. And Mother is standing there saying, "You have to die." Not just die eventually, but now—a sentence of death to take place now. That's all. A very stark little dream.

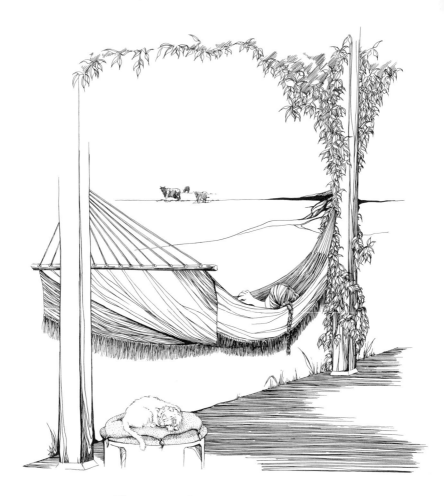

5 There *are* times in life when the things one
dreams and longs for actually come to pass.
There are periods of life remembered as Arcadia. For my children it was their grandmother's place.
For myself and my sisters, Arcadia was the summers we
spent at Rose Cottage with our aunts.

Mary and Alice Franklin left Kirkwood and went
to live in a little house on land across from my uncle's

dairy farm in Columbia, Missouri. They lived there all year round with kerosene lamps, wood and coal stoves before the electric power lines came, but we knew only the summer world, the vacation world of childhood.

The misty morning heat came across the pond by nine. Mist rising out of the huge ugly pond with its little pump house and its cattle-marked margin. Sometimes a pig lingered near the fence. Susan or Agamemnon. The morning sun opened the blue morning glories. Aunt Alice knelt in the strawberry bed weeding the wet garden. We didn't help much. Maybe she didn't really want us to. They wanted us to have fun, be happy, remember it all our lives. And we did, we did.

The strawberries. Small and sweet and red under the leaves. I must have eaten them, although the threat of hives hung over me. I remember stemming and sorting and sugaring them, and it seem unlikely I would have done it purely for someone else in those days. The martyr, the masochist, the spartan, did not develop for several years. At that time I was a simple pleasant, murderous child, still struggling with my limitations. Those real and those imagined, and those raining from above.

The fragrance of strawberries, a soaked piece of biscuit dough, rises up delicate and rich. Strawberries were not big and swollen and tasteless with a sweet slime cover then. The plastic cheesecake pie was not invented. Great plastic berries on a pale plastic pie covered with plastic cream.

I remember biscuits—big squashy delicious biscuits with homemade butter. The butter paddles were wood, the great bowl shaped like a canoe was made of wood. The churn was glass, and through it we could see the butter forming—that marvelous *event* happening before our eyes, the first gold flakes. In the butter bowl were salt and ice—the right amount of salt. It was a high art, a Franklin art. Aunt Alice knew exactly when to stop turning the churn handle—otherwise it all went back to a milky mush. (We did not like buttermilk in those days, the leftover flakes of butter gagged one.)

Aunt Mary in her fragile print dress, so clean, so clean, over her fragile little bones. Her thin hands and her smile. Aunt Mary slaving away for her nieces over a raging hot coal stove in midsummer, producing a long pageant of food . . . the memory of homemade rolls with cinnamon and raisins, angel food cake a foot high, fried chicken that makes one wonder what it is one eats today called chicken. An art that vanished as a play vanishes. Aunt Mary never ate much herself—a crumb of cake, a wing or neck of chicken, a bit of rind from the huge roasts when Uncle Vaughan and Aunt Edith came across the road to Sunday dinner.

Uncle Vaughan was venerated. "Vaughan says . . . ," "Vaughan thinks . . . ," and Vaughan Hickman was a man ahead of his time, a socialist, and a socialist who could not put theory into practice. An overpowering and quiet man, whose size and tongue and cynical smile frightened the child of a city businessman.

B. Tom used to come stamping into the little back porch on cold early mornings, bringing messages from Uncle Vaughan, receiving messages for Aunt Edith, or requests—I cannot imagine Aunt Mary ordering— or matters that concerned the north forty or for more chicken feed. B. Tom was a man and therefore interesting, but not to be spoken to. He came and went above our heads. And had a dark-blue wool cap on his own. Such as my son Terry came to wear and love. An extension of one's head and hair. One's magic. (As is my old gray beaked cap now. My comfortable familiar, protector of eyes, sharpener of vision, once lost and found again, wet, muddy, waiting patiently like a gray turtle under the ferns.)

B. Tom brought stove wood and piled it neatly on the back porch. Great black snakes would sometimes lie on the rafters and slip down the walls. The hand pump and the sink were there. No mechanism today can give me the feeling of triumph that water gushing from a hand pump gave.

Rubber boots were on the porch, and the aunts' big gray sweater hung on hooks. The burlap icebags were kept there neatly piled, and the harness hung on pegs —bridles and lead straps and blankets—but not the saddles. Curry combs and ointments for saddle sores.

And I remember summer storms.

Storms aren't what they used to be. They are violent when they come, but they do not have the ritual I remember from childhood. The slow and massive buildup of clouds, the lowering shapes, the lightning that flickered for hours ahead in the north, the heat and quiet, in which all the sweat in us, all the scents of the woods and the barns were pressed out like dew. And then there would be the first deceptive wind blowing *into* the storm, the darkness, and finally the fat separate drops of rain, big as cat feet at first, and then the down drenching avalanche of water, in which all drops were one.

Today the winds come high and light in the tree-tops, like the sweepings of someone else's storm. The sky is white, the leaves of the trees are white. The very rain is bleached out and old.

There is no sense now of future, of returning rhythm, as in those days. No sense of both the now and the future now. Again and again and again we knew the same marvelous things would happen. Again the purple clematis would bloom, big lovely purple stars, again the white fuzzy wall of white clematis, little white stars—again the dew on the grass, again the moonflowers opening white in the evening.

The moonflower memory. The moonflower event. Great floating white blooms, wide across as plates, with that exquisite night fragrance, faint powdery scent. You could watch—impatiently—that long closed trumpet with its sticky fur slowly unfurl, or you could run around the house and come back to see the miracle, the huge white blossom with its gold heart wide open in the thirty seconds you were gone. Better than morning glories, better than roses. Did you plant the moonflowers this year, Aunt Alice? . . . Will the moonflowers be there when we come? . . . Moonflowers grew on the little outhouse, always clean and with its small bucket of lime and its little trowel.

Memories of people move about too much. The angles change. But the dew on the grass, in the fresh bright morning hours—that stays, that memory does not shift and frown and look miles away with pain. The lovely smell of grass in the sun. The short grass that

Aunt Alice cut by herself with the little sharp hand mower . . . rattling rolling pushing . . . the sticky blades of green grass between one's wet sticky toes. And sandals, barefoot sandals, lovely shoes. Childhood and sandals (and all one could think about was the day one could wear high heels and patent-leather pumps).

But the dew on the grass in the fresh bright morning hours, that stays, that does not change.

203, first home of Benjamin and Ethel Johnson in Kirk-wood. Big trees and porch, barn in back.

Above, Family gathering on steps. Grandmother Harriet Johnson and Aunt Elizabeth Johnson in center. Dad serene in bowler hat. Miss Sallie Stevens above. Franklin sisters, Uncle Vaughan Hickman and daughter Jane in a circle around.

Opposite top, Josephine on pony, Bobby, with Father

Opposite bottom, Dad doing 4th of July fire tricks. Mary Elizabeth, Florence, Josephine watching. Miss Sallie at right.

"The next house was large and beautiful. When the aunts built 621 they saved the oak trees."

Barn, hammocks in back yard of 621

Aunt Laura sitting at the iris and lily pool before it was fenced

Josephine, ten years old

Rose Cottage, where we spent the happiest summers of our childhood with aunts in Columbia, Missouri

Opposite top, Alice and Mary Franklin in front of Rose Cottage

Opposite bottom, Josephine, Mary Lib, Cousin Jane and Florence, on farm, Columbia, Missouri

III

HILLBROOK
AND THE OLD HOUSE

6 In 1883 when the Franklins moved from the suburbs of St. Louis to their new home in Kirkwood, the land around it was largely country, a place of woods and trees, large houses, farms and long winding shady roads. In my childhood it was still a leafy, tree-lined town, but no longer country. In 1922 my own parents conceived, as Aunt Florence had put it, their own brilliant plan of moving to the country, and

my father bought a farm and sold his wholesale coffee business in St. Louis. (I can still smell the harsh sweet fragrance of raw coffee, see the brown beans sliding down troughs, and the big rolltop desk in Dad's office, the boats on the Missouri River, the big stones of the levee.) Mother was tired of trees, she wanted a view, and they built the house, a big stone house, on the top of a naked hill, not a tree around, and you could see the lights of St. Louis fifteen miles away. Dad was sixty years old and had worked very hard all his life. He had dreamed of this retirement for many years.

He had a little while of his dream. Grapevines and cows and corn and horses and a good man to do the work. He named the place Hillbrook, a pleasant homely name for the pleasant life he hoped to live. He had money and leisure now, but his health was gone. He had put the dream off too long. In a few short years he died of cancer.

Twenty years is a long time in one place. I loved that place. I knew every inch of it, and every hour of the day and every season. But I have no will to write about it now. Too much pain. Too long ago. Growing up is a terrible time. A person lives with such intensity you wonder there is anything left to go on with when it's over. It's a life assimilated now, used up, written out. A curious life. Mother was left with four girls, two hundred acres, and four living sisters of her own. We all turned out strangely sane in spite of everything, although we wondered sometimes if we would make it. There was lots of sky. I saw more sky there on the farm than ever in my life before. Sky and wind. I had a rolltop desk in the attic under a dormer window (the wind through those dormer windows made an eerie banshee sound), and I wrote. I wrote, if not endlessly, then enormously, fulsomely. I seemed to be waiting to begin to live; and not all the beauty, all the intensity of the words on paper, not all the public actions, all the desperate search for reform and change, the bitterness of the depression years, not the love for my sisters nor the tortuous refining of a personal philosophy, seemed to be the reality of living that I wanted to find. And then I met Grant Cannon and the waiting-to-live was over and the real life began.

Grant came to St. Louis from Salt Lake City, from that valley surrounded by mountains and deserts, where one lives in the presence of mountains, and lives in the presence of pioneer ancestors from the hour of birth. How can I write about what made him Grant? The subject is too enormous. Grant was born into the Mormon Church and it colored all his life, even though he left it when he was eighteen. He was the grandson of the pioneer George Q. Cannon, and that is not something lightly left behind. He showed me his own home in Salt Lake City, and his grandfather's many houses for his wives. But Grant begins with Brigham Young saying, "This is the Place," and Grant's own long search for Place, which he found as much as any man will ever find.

He came to St. Louis by way of San Francisco, where he had arrived by freight car and hobo camps in search of work and had got a job under WPA. By the time he reached St. Louis he was working for the National Labor Relations Board as a field examiner, and we met in a courtroom in those days when the unions were young and revolutionary and a force for change.

I have lived a long part of my life in other people's houses. Too long. Some people do not really grow up, do not leave their childhood until they live in a house of their own. Grant was drafted in the beginning of World War II and spent almost four years of his life in the Army and I went on living in Mother's house. But it was literally my birthday, that April more than a quarter of a century ago, when Grant and I were married in Mother's house. It was Easter day that year, very warm, with all the flowering bushes in bloom. Spirea in showers, crocus in the grass. It was an extraordinary spring and from that hour I was married to an extraordinary man for thirty years. A man who built himself, faults, talents, wounds and virtues, into a work of amazing art. No, the word is *human*. Alive and mortal. Human without end.

When the war was over and Grant came back, we wanted a place, a house, a home of our own. And all those years, all those other places, do not seem as real as the Old House in Newtown, Ohio, where Grant and I and the children came to live in 1947. It was the first house that either of us had ever owned.

When we bought this house, built in 1810 of bricks made of clay from the valley's earth, we bought a homestead with a history that went back more than a hundred and thirty years. The place had great maple trees, a swamp, an icehouse ruined and covered with ivy, a huge second building with a smokehouse, a view of alfalfa fields and corn, and the endless surflike sound of the quarry pits—at that time, a half mile away.

The old house was beautiful and majestic in the way that houses never are anymore. And it was also in need of eternal vigilance, as are old and crumbling people, beautiful and majestic though they be in age. It was inhabited by memories and by insects, by bats, by mice, and rats and odd noises. The first year that we came to this house of fourteen wandering rooms on different levels, the mercury in winter went down to five below zero every night, and the silent icy air flowed quietly as a river through the gray brick walls. Apparently choosing, like water, the path of least resistance. Like old people with great virtues and innumerable weakness acquired by time, the old house had aged, crumbled here and there continually, talked a good deal to itself at night. I wore mittens and galoshes and a woolen cap in the kitchen that first winter, and at last we put a blower in the furnace so that the leisurely currents of the fire might reach at least the floors of the bedrooms far away in the upper regions.

The children, Terry nine then and Annie six, grew accustomed to the vast uncoziness of all the rooms, to the height space which equaled the floor space. Were one to have painted a moon on the ceiling, there would seem to be no roof at all. I think now their souls grew in proportion to the unlimited freedom of their ceiling skies. Those old walls spoke. The floors spoke. There was a crack in the floor above the furnace. You could lie on the boards and look down on Terry and Grant in the cellar, pulling out burned slag, the fiery coal wreaths from the furnace. There was a tremendous satisfaction in hooking a wreath intact—turning it sidewise and jerking it through the door unbroken. Where it lay—a great black cooling doughnut. Then came the leap of the flames released inside, and the heat pouring upward through the pipes even to the remote bedrooms far far overhead. Those fifteen-foot ceilings. Those tremendous rooms . . . We were never warm in winter, and even in March the fog, frozen on the trees during the night, dripped like rain in the morning. The small icy drops fell on the cold grass, hung and glittered from the blue-grass ghosts. The birds were restless, the starlings made shuffling, untimely motions of mating among the cold wet branches. The moss on the dead redbud tree was a bright gold-green, and the sparrows were everywhere, jabbering and bouncing, calling on God to notice their near-escapes, and preparing to sparrow the earth with their subdividing selves.

The air was clear and raw between weathery days, the sky barren and immensely far away. As though the dome had retreated. The slow fight for life between the hyacinths, the daffodils, and the freezing nights bronzed the shoot tips and gave them a stunted and sullen but tenacious look. There may have been no substance left in them for flowers, but they were determined not to die. The pines and cedars emerged from their yellow dull-ness, that jaundiced winter look which is usually painted as a brilliant green in the artist's winter scene.

When I am cold I can think of nothing but being cold. All the clever and cunning pathways of the mind are occupied solely by clever and cunning—and usually clumsy—schemes and machinations to get warm. Like a thin-haired dog, the mind rushes frantically about, huddling in doorways of nothingness and trembling with misery, and the mortal flesh crouches over the radiator, adds wool socks, puts hands in pockets, hovers over the stove burners, and longs for spring. As well try to cook a potato in ice water as conceive fine—or even tolerable—thoughts in a cold house. I hated coldness with a plain, beautiful hatred. It could say nothing good for itself. I could frighten myself blue by merely looking at a picture of a walrus on an ice cake. Hairless, fish-eyed, ready to plunge into glacial waters and sink miles into cold, frozen purity of water, arctic water, sea-green, ice-blue, glacier-white ocean water . . .

But the old house was full of life. All kinds of life.

Grant had a vision of making corncobs into nourishing chicken feed. The "guest room" at the Old House, which was both cool and sunny, held at times a huge chicken-wire cage full of ground cobs. The old cellar held glass jars full of urea. The cage was moved about to ventilate and ripen the treated cobs. I cannot remember the addition of molasses, though—molasses so essential to the making of cobs into feed for cattle. The cage shed little bits of cob, but nothing sticky. It stood all winter upstairs, moved about according to the weather. The room above the kitchen had no heat. It was piled with magazines. All the magazines we bought and saved were piled end to end—the great wall of China had nothing on our building blocks. Terry sorted them one day when he was nine, according to their size and kind, and then he said with triumph, "It's all done, and all your what-is-the-world-coming-to pamphlets are in a separate pile." The world has come to all that now. There is nothing it has not come to. Or will come. All that the dusty little books cried out in anguish against, in that cold room.

But Grant would not go down under that barrage of horror. "I cannot bear not to hope. I cannot live without hope." And he made no lifelong truce with despair as I have made.

The chickens pecked at the cobs in a perfunctory sort of way. The experiment was not a scientific breakthrough, only a sort of cracking of the crust, you might say, as that delicate movement of the earth and shuddering of grass proves that a mole is working.

Grant played the flute. He sang. I loved to hear him sing. Not the sticky and romantic. (What is the borderline? Where in the semicircular canals, the brain, is the borderline in each human head between the syrup and that transcendent sense of soaring, or the fiery stir of sex?) I loved to hear him sing. The Mormon hymn "Though long to you that journey may appear . . . ," that was beautiful—and all the familiar Christmas songs and the church hymns of my childhood, they really got me, sent me. One is a computer. Punch this. Pull that. It embarrassed the cool mind. It does not embarrass me today. It is life. Life is more than that cool lump.

He loved the children passionately. He loved them almost too much. They needed a cooler climate. That's hard for parents to understand. But my fault with the children was not a too tropical climate, too much sun, but a climate of apprehension, the expectation of coming storms (storms that did not come), dark clouds on far horizons feared. (It was always hard for me to keep from watering the cactus plants. My cactus always died of root rot.)

"I learned to be an optimist just in reaction to gloomy people," Annie said. Annie who came trailing clouds of glory from heaven if ever a child did. If I could live those years again! But I cannot live those years again.

March is the month of negotiations and promises. Of sudden warm winds and unexpected greenness. One bitter day I found the snowdrops in bloom and nearly fell down on my knees. The pure and waxy drops hung white and perfect above the tired old grass, unharmed, almost unaware of the frosty raw air around them. When I brought them in they opened wide at once in the warmth. The grackles felt the spring and I saw two fighting in the grass—one of the most vicious things I have ever seen. They hunted for each other's eyes in a hail of blue-black wings, and stabbed and pounded as though they held daggers, and their claws scratched each other's brittle legs and they clung in a frenzy of slippery feathers. They whirled over and over, and lay still in exhaustion, and then stabbed again. This went on and on until suddenly a whole flock of birds flew over, their shadows like rain over the grass and over the frantic fighters, and with a single squawking cry they parted and flew away.

The cat Minx came of age and felt the spring. Such frenetic contortions and unhappy compulsions. And the other, Monstro, silent, childlike, spent most of his time in fat furry sleep. While mangy yellow cats, gray cats like shadows, cats one never saw before, came and went furtively by day and night.

But the power of the dying winter in March is still manifest and strong. The bitter king rules by fear, for, even rheumy-eyed and hoarse, it is known he can still rise as a giant in the night. Unloved, unforgiven, his ice-locked lands disintegrating beyond his power, he is still king. We should have festivals here in March, such as in Europe years ago, when mock battles between Winter and Summer were fought in the villages to assist the coming in of spring. And the figure of Winter, wrapped in furs with an ice shovel in his mittened hands, was traditionally defeated by a more fortunate fellow townsman chosen for Spring, and adorned with boughs and flowers. How much more appropriate in March than in May to have such a festival, when all the evidence of the old king's power lies about us in the snowy fields, and the cold crows fly overhead, and the wind shakes the glass and assails the very bricks of the house. Think then of our streets—or even one portion of a street—with all the telephone poles twined with pink paper roses and purple violets made by the schoolchildren; and the solitary figure of King Winter, mounted or on foot, depending on whether the local mayor can ride or not, wrapped in a raccoon coat and a muff on his head, and carrying a monstrous papier-mâché icicle, marching down among the festive poles. And then, suddenly, he sees the flower- and leaf-crowned person of Spring, small (but wiry), with a vine-wrapped pole, advancing bravely through the grimy snow, followed by a fluttering crowd of white-clad third-grade children, all carrying the biggest bright-est flowers that glue pot and scissors could devise, and garlanded arches overhead. And their white robes long enough to hide galoshes on their feet. Then comes the battle between Life and Death, between old Winter and Spring; and the mayor is driven to his knees, his icicle shattered in a thousand pasty paper parts, his beard is held in Spring's tight adolescent grasp, and he begs for mercy as the little ones surround him, singing, with their hoops of flowers. Think how the promise of warmth and light and the blooming orchards would seem more cer-tain, as we, who are watchers in this rite, see Winter's muff pulled from his head, a crown of leaves placed on his shivering baldness, and down some convenient local alley the old King scuttles ignominiously away, while children strew the chilly streets with their blazing flowers.

One April Fools' Day at the old house, the children set out with bamboo poles, tramped through the beds of purple violets, and went fishing among the branches of the apple tree. And in that spring this was no trick upon the fishing children, but on the great carp themselves that swam bewildered among the leafing branches. Part of the land dipped down suddenly into a small swamp full of maple trees and willows and one ancient apple tree. And each spring this low-lying hollow filled up with water; and in flood years, the river itself moved up the road and into our land. It was a curious sight to see the cornfields sheeted in gray water, and the invisible inching of the water coming up the road, like a giant amoeba feeling its way, and all above the serene, faint blue of the untroubled sky. And the delicate flowering branches of the plum and the pattern of red elm haloes were reflected in water that once had been the land.

The waters drained very sluggishly back into the river when the flood was over, and by late April the brown pools were covered with elm seeds and maple wings, and full of fat pulpy tadpoles swimming in and out of the dappled light. There is something curious and wonderful about the thought of an independent embryo, alive and alert and on its own, carrying its adult self within, the child being father to the man indeed, and giving it out charily—a foot emerging here, a childish tail disappearing, and then the final unveiling of the green and gold and umber frog-shaped dampness, with bright humped-up eyes.

Some of the tadpoles were stranded in drying pools, and the children rescued them in jars, carried them up the slippery mudbank, and let the little monsters loose in a washtub filled with dark-smelling swamp water. The tadpole did not prosper well in captivity, and not many days passed before the inevitable blue body would float up to the surface with closed eyes, and the air was full of the brackish smell of tadpoles poaching in the sun.

Sometimes the world of our shrunken oasis became too familiar and scanty, and it would have been pleasant to sit in the apple tree above the swamp and see instead of drying mud a hippopotamus rising from the shallows, or the tall unearthly weaving of giraffes among the crowded maples. Or to know that the sound one heard would bring the bright baboons in sight, and not the neighbors' children.

But the coming of the spring is enough of newness, enough of the strange, for even all the expected things carry the never-failing glamour of rebirth, and the very weeds, so monstrous later, have the tender light of immortality around them still. April is the perfect month, a month of almost too exact appropriateness for the bringing of children into the world. An April baby is surrounded by images of itself in all the various half-opened flowers and tree buds, wet emerging butterflies and moist wriggling tadpoles in the shallow water. The perfect packaging of a baby is more astounding than even the satin wrappings of the hickory and chestnut buds which swell gradually and break their smooth and waxy sheaths. Carol came firmly packed and plump as a loaf of bread, although some children even at six weeks look weak and wrinkled like white soggy moths or little toadstools; and, though since the beginning of man's time babies have been born into the world, a child seems as incredible and new as the first bubble that rose and breathed when the oceans drew back from the land.

The voice of a new child has an odd springlike sound (even the high wailing notes more piercing than needles) and in the first year it runs the gamut of all the bird and new young animal voices, from the muttering of the pigeons and the pure rounded notes of the dove to the harsh crowing of the young rooster and the barking of a puppy. And a baby even growls softly when it pounces on an unwary piece of toast.

Stacked up beside a month-old kitten or a puppy, a baby seems too naked, and much in need of fur; but given time it will outstrip them, and prove the quickly given charm of fur and paws only a transitory thing.

Life was very rich. Grant's mind reminded me of an electric powerhouse full of various engines. He went about revving them up and down, attending to them, neglecting them, returning—but none ever went cold. In the editorship of the magazine he became knowledgeable about an enormous number of things. Knowledgeable—but, more important, really interested. He was a fine photographer, as well as writer and editor. He had appreciation of art, of music, of food (and was a splendid cook), of nature, of psychology, of human foibles and human greatness. He had variety and yet such steadfastness! Medicine, politics, religion, mathematics—all these fascinated him. I am hard put to think of a subject that bored him. Human beings, their actions and reactions endlessly absorbed him, although he was not always aware of what lies under what lies under. . . . He tried to really learn the craft of things. He was a skilled amateur. He tried pottery, movies, plays. He had imagination and understanding and visions. He was always trying to understand man in relation to this incredible universe. . . . He was always trying. . . . Grant looked for hope. He looked for light. You have to *look*. He tried and he kept on trying. I suppose his own nature was with him instead of against him. But still he could have gone down under if he hadn't tried. And he made me into a human being, too. Out of something more sea grass and sand.

Nothing accomplished was enough. What do you want, I'd ask. I don't know. . . . He should have remembered what happens to overfertilized waters when he kept saying, "It is not enough. I haven't succeeded. I want to do more." And more and more.

During all the years of his work on *The Farm Quarterly*, a job of incredible weight and variety, he was also doing a thousand other things. It seemed as though he wanted to live everything in life. He got a pilot's license and flew a plane himself—until one time he came very close to death in a fog. He joined the Friends Meeting, and when he took part in the entertainments the Meeting gave the patients at Longview Hospital and was not satisfied that this was accomplishing all that could be done, he had himself admitted and lived with the patients in the wards, he wrote a report about this and then a play. The play, *Samuel* . . . It expressed some of his own inner torments—that hidden life which he kept down better than I did. It was—is—a good play, strong and dramatic, but he did not know how to end it. He was too honest to fake the powerful and uplifting conclusion that it needed. That conclusion was something one could not bring about simply by hard gritty patient work such as he did on his book *Great Men of Agriculture*. My God, he answered 533 questions of fact or revision—five hundred and thirty three queries—and did it with that magnificent patient rage. Sometimes he swore, sometimes he laughed, but he did it.

We joked about honesty and the heart's secret desire to overleap it. To believe that fortune cooky, that small pink slip uncoiled to say, "You will be successful in everything you do."

We loved that moment of opening the dry folded dough in the booth Sunday noon after Meeting. The good and inexpensive food, the teacups, Carol's lovely face. Unstarved at last. The sweet-sour morsels gone. The little mounds of rice vanished. On the walls bright pink and red paintings. Grant felt especially good if he had spoken in Meeting and said something out of his heart and mind both. A rare conjunction for any of us. The essence of the place was our intolerable hunger, the proprietor's black-haired children at a little table near the desk, the rice balls both sticky and separate-grained, and the fortune cookies: "You will be fortunate in a love affair," "Your investments will be good." . . .

They were always messages of an uplifting sort, of good cheer. But only once was that pink coil of paper of such transcendent augury, and Grant got it. "You will be successful in everything you do."

In a sense this was true. The success was in the trying, in the doing. In the living to the ultimate of one's desire and capacity.

I drove him wild with my vision of beginning again. Selling everything, giving everything away, canceling insurance, burning the house. Go live in a one-room shack in the woods. Save only the land—and our own souls. It denied the validity of everything he had worked for. The citizen of a community, with roots in the social, financial, philanthropic, arts and business circles. The power structure. Security for old age and sickness. He looked back on his own family and the many lives that went into his own and he wanted a sense of place and continuity.

The conventional forms of recognition pleased him. He deserved them more than a lot of men. He was in *Who's Who*. His book *Great Men of Modern Agriculture* was published and still sells. He became the editor of *The Farm Quarterly*. A member of the Cincinnati Literary Club . . . Nothing was enough. (I wonder if he knew that prizes, clubs, honors, began to seem archaic relics to his children, trinkets and paper crowns of a dying culture.) He grew, he was growing all his life. He would have grown beyond the need for paper crowns.

April is the most dependable of all months. Unfailingly cold and damp and beautiful. I can recall no year in which the promise has been broken. No year in which the miracle of wild white plums in fragrant clouds has not materialized and been frozen in a trance by some of the rawest, nastiest air that ever descended from the white regions of outer space. No year in which I have not seen the red flowers of the Judas tree through the fall of a shockingly cold rain. And no year in which there has not been one day-of-God, in which all things are perfect for twelve breathtaking hours, and not one leaf is eaten by the worm.

On such a day I found the wild pink crab trees blooming on a hillside with the gnarled hawthorns, each separate as though planted in an orchard, with no other trees. Each short and perfect and fragrant, like a field of rose-and-white bouquets, and in the sun the odor was drawn out until it was a warm blanket of spice and perfume over all the field.

On the twigs and crotches of the twisted branches of each crab and hawthorn a thrush had built its twiggy nest, and on each nest sat a long-tailed, fierce-eyed thrush of the tree beside it. So that the hillside was like a design repeated over and over—a warm, pink-and-white patch of wallpaper stretched out underneath the sky.

And on the next day a sleet-cold rain came down over the field of blossoms, mashed the pink petals into the grass, and April was wholly faithful to us, in her fashion.

Along with the usual spring ant armies, and the sparrows' bulging feathery nests, one April brought us one of the strangest nocturnal tenants since the ousting of the bat colony under the roof, and it is to be remembered unlovingly as the Month of the Flower-loving Rat. This strange creature lived in the porous bricks of the ancient fireplace (boarded up now and never used—lighting a fire there being something like tampering with the respiratory tract of an ancient and crumbling old lady), and for a long time we never saw him, only heard the sound of his teeth at night, slowly fletcherizing the brick and plaster.

Rats had come before. One night in desperation Terry and I chased one with an axe in the cellar. Around and around it fled, always scraping the stone walls. We could not kill it. It was not a good thing to have tried to do. One night I found a sick young rat in the kitchen drawer. Took drawer and rat outside in the freezing night and, standing on a pile of frozen newspapers (wet from soaking the spill of some broken pipe inside), killed it. And the cat caught five young rats one night on the cold side porch. It seemed necessary to kill a good deal in the country. Wild cats, rats, sparrows, chickens. One should think of this squarely, face to face with sixty years behind one. So I killed. So what? But that won't do.

I drowned kittens. Drowned a sparrow's nest once. Killed chickens to eat. Sick rabbits (whose guts spilled warbles big as hickory nuts). But Grant did most of it. "It's too hard on you," he said. I must have made audible —visible—distress. So, he did it. He was always doing things for me. Sparing me. One never knows how much went on inside. What torment he took to himself. Or whether it was really easier for him, as he claimed. I think he had a greater capacity to draw on. A greater love of life which is a physical thing when you come down to it. Man is an ocean inside, they say. Maybe Grant was born with more nutrients, living tides of internal refreshment. We are all different. Some with hearts bigger, livers smaller, kidneys upside down, adrenal glands sidewise. Decisions of life or death made by madmen with screwed-up pituitaries.

We first became aware of this curious rat when a vase of plum blossoms quite out of reach of anything not two feet high was knocked over on the floor, and a trail of white petals led from the dwindling pool to the fireplace, and the twigs were left carelessly strewn there as though for burning. The next time it was tulips, the first lavender and waxy-lemon flowers from the garden, placed on a bookcase four feet high, but reached in the night, tipped over and carried back to the fireplace. Not eaten, mind you, but *arranged* at the front door of his hidden home. And after the tulips, the white narcissus were lifted from their vase—not the green leaves, but the pure white blossoms—and the vase, quite undisturbed, stood in the center of the dining-room table, with three flowers still remaining, a flower balanced lightly on the table edge, and the rest in the fireplace.

"It must be an agouti," we said when the plum blossoms fell, but then the tulips came down, and with the narcissus strange images began to come to us. A Thing growing night after night in some other-world response to the increasing height of the flower vases. Nothing stopped it. Not even the *top* of the five-foot bookcase from which he extracted the April lilacs and took them to his den. No doubt to adorn a special occasion, the anniversary of some April witch to whom he served polished chicken bones and prussic acid from stolen peach seeds.

We were afraid of using poison, knowing how untenable the house had become for weeks when even a mouse had died in the honeycombed walls, but we set traps and looked at them warily in the mornings, there being a time when the hunter begins to fear the hunted, but nothing was ever found inside. We had caught rats in these traps before, ordinary, stolid, food-loving rats who climbed up on top of the icebox, brought down the bread slice by slice and reassembled it under the icebox, but not rats in league with Something Else—not winged rodents.

Finally came the day when we said we must try

poison, but first we tried, without hope, one final gesture. A loose brick opening led to the ash box below the fireplace—completely sealed in the cellar for no known reason, and a fitting place for a rat to nap in. We decided to seal this over above, but first, in order not to entomb him like a heretic, we threw down some burning paper to drive him forth, and waited a reasonable interval—reasonable for any natural thing, at least—of hours, before we cemented the floor of the fireplace up.

We said, to my knowledge at least, no mystic words, the smoke from the burning paper appeared a normal choking smoke, no rat appeared, no sound was heard, but from that day on our tenant was no longer with us. The dark was silent, the apple blossoms shed their petals of their own accord, and one night I set the first gold roses on a stool and left them there till dawn, and not one rose had been disturbed. The ritual of fire had exorcised him when all else had failed.

7 Like the night, an old house has a thousand eyes. Small shapes and forms have inhabited it from generation to generation. When one comes to live in such a house, one must expect small unwinking eyes in the darkness; the cracks in the floor, the knotholes in the wood, the ancient beams of the cellar, have a life of their own. There is the loud tick of the wood beetle, the soundless scurry of the centipede

like a furry shadow, and the sudden appearance of black ant borings around the kitchen sink.

But there were also certain tenants that no one told us about at all.

The enormous house was beautiful, and its cost had been reasonable, much more reasonable than that of a house of normal size—a rare and capricious combination. In addition there were three acres around it, and at the back door a tall and crumbling brick structure, big as another house, which had been used as the servants' quarters long ago. We had bought all this and moved in at Christmas time. Not until April were we aware that we were no longer alone, and that, added to all the registered members of the family and the migratory assorted insect life, up from their southern wintering spa had come the tenants of over a hundred years, the enormous summer colony of the *Fledermäuse*, the *chauves-souris* —in the colder English, bats.

The extent of this homecoming was not apparent to us all at once. We began to be aware of bats drifting out from under the eves at twilight, swooping to and fro under the southern porch and then scattering high over the cornfields, weaving long swinging patterns until they were lost, invisible in the night.

"The bat is an insect eater," I said. "Bats help keep the balance of nature, and therefore are very good things to have around." "Balance of nature" had a comforting sound, but one evening when standing in peace, admiring the magnificent silhouette of our great brick mansion against the sky, we became aware that the comet-like streak of bat after bat from the narrow eaves had been going on for a long, long time.

"You sit on this side of the house and count," Grant said, "I'll take the other side." His voice had a curious, strained sound.

For a little while I sat in silence and counted. Fifty bats went by. Fifty more. I got tired of counting and just watched the streakings and swoopings, undiminished in number or timing, go on and on.

After a while Grant came back with a look that seemed clearly dark and thoughtful, even in the dim twilight gloom. "And how many did *you* count?" he asked. His voice was that of one who graciously withholds his news, knowing its nature can never be topped or spoiled.

I said I'd only counted a hundred but that they'd kept coming on and on.

"I counted one thousand three hundred and seventy-three!" he said. "Good God! Why do you suppose nobody ever *told* us?"

Bats were still flowing out from under the eaves.

As June warmed into July a mousy smell like musky mignonette became a palpable presence. It filled the upper rooms thick as a furry fog and started to creep softly and smotheringly down the stair. And then the bats themselves, a few of the finally estimated four thousand, began coming *inside* the house. Their small restless shapes would appear suddenly, swooping across a lighted room. From the cracks around sills, from supposedly sealed fireplaces, and from God knows where, they crept forth, and a long, curiously unforgettable summer had begun.

In the wonderful *Illustrated Natural History of the Animal Kingdom* by S. G. Goodrich, which I referred to in this trying time, published in 1859 and full of amazing lore and truly horrendous etchings of the Bat Megaderm and the Bat Rhinolophus Nobilis (size of life), there appeared these memorable sentences:

> In a rude age, the imagination needs little encouragement to convert objects so really curious and strange as those we have been describing, into hideous monsters, endowed with supernatural powers. It is the province of education and enlightened reason to reduce these horrid creations of fancy to the comparatively simple and innocent dimensions of truth.

Now, Grant, educated and enlightened though he was, may be described as a brave man who abhorred bats. With his abhorrence herein reached all the climax of their conflicting powers—beyond which man neither can nor is expected to go. As twilight of each evening drew on, he would fetch the kitchen broom, place it close at hand and, with his back against the wall, relax nervously and begin to read. By the front door we kept an empty wastebasket and a flat cooky tin. We did not often have long to wait. A soundless shadow would speed across the light, casting its signature athwart the page; Grant would leap up with the broom and the evening was begun.

The radar mechanism of the bat is such that he avoids all obstacles in *front* with unerring accuracy. On the wing he is not likely to touch anything he does not wish to devour. (This is hard to believe, of course, and it is next to impossible to convince the white-faced guest that the low slicing dive which fans his cheek and lifts his hair is a deliberate miss, and not a deliberate attack that failed.) After some trial and error and considerable sweat, Grant learned to outwit the radar warning by swinging at the bat from *behind*, fouling its control mechanisms, as he put it, and speeding it into the nearest wall, where it bumped, folded, and fell to the floor. Then the wastebasket would be inverted over it, the cooky tin slipped under the wastebasket, and the whole borne hastily out the front door. One evening I released the lid too soon; the bat turned around and scuttled back into the house on its elbows, and had to be swept out again.

Several times I was awakened at night by the sense of a presence in the room, and once, stumbling to find the light, I stepped on a soft-furred thing that squirmed under my bare foot. Other furred things with wings swept back and forth across the room an inch or two above Grant's innocent sleeping face. He was a sound sleeper and did not wake while I furiously beat the air with his shirt and finally drove them into the darkness of the upper hall and quietly shut the door. In the morning I found them snuggled between the curtain folds and upside down on the shades.

It is almost impossible to convey the largeness, the oldness, the vulnerability of an ancient house, the small-ness, the craftiness, the dexterity of a bat. Convinced that they were coming inside through the windowsills of an upper room (during the day we could hear them talk-ing to each other inside the hollow wood), we hired a carpenter who came unhappily, removed the window frame and sill, announced it had been impossible for bats to get in from the outside and replaced the boards, sealed it all up—and the bats continued to enter.

Reports of our unusual number of what Mr. Goodrich describes as "one of the most remarkable groups in the whole circle of animated nature" began to circulate in Cincinnati, and two naturalist friends expressed what seemed to us a somewhat unnatural eagerness to go up under the roof, look around for themselves, and study the vespertilionidae *in situ*. Bearing a tremendous amount of camera equipment and a stout cotton bag, Karl Maslowski and Woody Goodpastor arrived one humid Saturday morning and disappeared cheerfully up the small trapdoor in the ceiling. They ranged about in the hot fragrant darkness for some time. For quite a long time, in fact, and sometimes they were very quiet. Another fragment from Mr. Goodrich's book began to haunt me with its gentle incisiveness. "In India," he wrote, "the megaderms may be heard on quiet evenings crunching the heads and bones of frogs." But eventually the men returned with about sixty bats in the bag and the heartening report that the old manse probably contained the largest concentration of bats in the world outside of the Carlsbad Caverns. We sat awhile meditatively on the front porch, drank iced coffee, and watched the bag undulate and nearly walk off by itself.

As a naturalist Karl took only a calm, detached view of the situation. Woody, who had worked for exterminating companies, remarked that no company would guarantee a bat job, but that they might try— for a price. The thought of actually exterminating four thousand bats, not just driving them away, was truly appalling to me.

On the other hand, if we merely drove them out, there was always the great brick servants' quarters for their refuge, open to sun and wind, impossible to seal, too expensive to demolish, and but a few paces from the back door, where the gentlest breeze could bring the musky presence right back into the house again. Karl and Woody were sympathetic about our unusual problem; told us to be of good cheer, that the bats would leave with the first frost sometime in October; and after a while swung the bag into the car and went home to stuff bats and develop some excellent pictures of the attic.

A few weeks passed. Friends who used to drop in began quietly staying away. Then one sweltering summer day, impelled by duty, Grant determined to carry this fragmentary battle to the very stronghold under the roof itself, drive out the bats once and for all, and sell the guano to connoisseurs in the garden clubs. His plan was simple, and based on close, if not loving, observation of the creatures' nocturnal habits. At ten in the evening, long after the working hours of the bats had started, he would go up with a bright light. This would drive away any of the more home-loving type who might have expected to spend the evening in.

12 P.M.: Go up and light two sulphur candles.

4:30 to 5 A.M.: Bats return, smell sulphur, and go—elsewhere.

4 P.M.: Grant to go up into dark attic (now to be

free of sulphur fumes and all bats), plug up holes with aid of light shining in from outside, and problem is solved.

The plan began on schedule at ten o'clock. Grant dressed himself carefully in his old army clothes, tucked the pants legs into combat boots, put on a pair of bee-keeper's gloves that came up over his shirtsleeves, and then carefully placed over his head a paper bag in which he had cut two eyeholes sealed with clear cellophane. He than buttoned on another shirt (to keep the mammals from coming up under the bag), and climbed the ladder up to the trapdoor, beyond which lay, Mr. Goodrich had assured us, only "the simple and innocent dimensions of truth." The opening of the trapdoor let down a staggeringly warm wave of truth, but Grant silently struggled through and stood up with his light.

It was at this point that the plan began to disintegrate. In the first place, more bats like to stay in at night than you would imagine. Disturbed by the glare and sound, dozens of furry bodies let go of the beams and started swirling insanely around and around in the narrow space. Some opened their mouths and snarled and the pinkness showed up quite clearly, outlined by their little pointed teeth. The bat has a peculiar cry which can only be described as a chitter or at times a horrendous smacking kiss. Chittering and kissing, the bats swirled about with no apparent intention of being driven forth to feed in the cool starlight outside.

Nevertheless, Grant decided to go ahead, step up the procedure by lighting the sulphur candles now, and drive them all out at once. This he did, placing them in pans of water to keep the whole house from burning up, and descended the ladder.

In the gray dawn I went out, expecting to find the outside of the house a mass of fluttering wings and frustrated *Fledermäuse*. But there was not a bat in sight. At 4 P.M. (we, at least, kept to *our* part of the plan) we discovered that the sulphur had neither driven them away entirely nor kept them entirely from returning. It had, in fact, suffocated a certain selected number.

The smell of dead bats, live bats, and sulphur descended heavily throughout the house. Two days later, for the last time, a grim, tight-lipped man dressed in his airtight suit ascended the ladder bearing a bucket, twenty pounds of naphtha flakes to further discourage and repel the bats, and a bottle of pine-oil deodorant to drown the smell. Fighting his way among swirling and snarling little shapes, he collected all the bodies he could find, spread out the naphtha flakes—mainly by throwing balls of them at the bats—splashed pine oil over the rafters, and lowered the bucket of dead ones down through the door. (I buried them in the potato patch and was amazed at how light is even a whole bucketful of bats.) Then Grant came down, sealed up the trapdoor, and removed the ladder to the toolhouse. Something in his kindly open nature had hardened and his eyes had the withdrawn and distant look of those who have known some experiences not communicable to mortal men.

The summing up of that summer's efforts was an

unpleasant old house, redolent with naphtha, pine oil, sulphur, live bats, and dead bats. Bats were distributed about uncomfortably behind shutters, bats in hollow pillars of the porch, and most of the bats up under the roof where they had always been.

This was in August. We sat down in exhaustion and waited for the first sharp breath of frost to send them south.

The whole winter passed, in which we spoke sporadically of "doing something" about them. We thought of having a carpenter come who would go up and stop up every hole inside and out, a task of microscopic research and patience. But we did not know what the spring would then bring forth. Perhaps a house *completely* decorated with fur-lined shutters, or a brick bat-roost at the back door, or— Knowing the nature of the bat, a nightmare thought occurred to me: they would find one hole, one infinitesimal hole up under the eaves, and all four thousand would enter in the spring, and every night all four thousand would line up in a long, sinuous queue from beam to beam and, chittering and shoving, make their exit from that one hole, and in the gray dawn similarly return.

Thus April was upon us and the mass immigration took place again and nothing had been done to keep them out—and nothing could have been—and all that was left was the chance of professional mass extermination. It is difficult to explain, wholly apart from the costliness of such a thing, the moral scruples involved. Four thousand bats is a lot of life, and for a long time I could not bring myself to sanction such a sweeping and drastic destruction. They were just too many to be killed. For two months I temporized, delayed, hoped that this year would be different, better; but by June things were obviously the same—and worse. The walls might as well have been completely porous as far as the bats were concerned. We came to dread the gathering darkness, and not a single evening passed without at least two and sometimes four swooping shadows moving from room to room. Sometimes they held off until eleven, giving us false hopes of a peaceful night, but always and invariably before the stroke of midnight they were there.

We could not stand it any longer and we hardened our hearts. We called an exterminating company and had them make an estimate, but this was only the beginning.

The exterminator estimator said that the old end plates should be torn from the roof and replaced with new snug end plates—replaced after the brickwork had been pointed up to seal the place. We called a carpenter, an enormous fellow, who came, looked, and said that there was no sense mending the end plates until the gutters were repaired; so he called a tinsmith. The tinsmith said that he could not repair the gutters until the carpenter had torn off the molding. At this point, the carpenter revealed that he had grown too fat for ladder work and called in a subcarpenter who climbed up on the roof and reported that the molding was the gutter, and the gutter was a solid, hand-carved beam made from a single cedar and forty-five feet long without a break other than the rotten spot objected to by the tin-smith. The larger carpenter—who turned out to be more in the nature of a broker or procurer—said to chop it down anyway. And on a hot June morning the sub and smaller carpenter actually began to saw and chop, and the last and final ousting of the tenants began.

The great rotting gutter came down in sections, the carpenter reported there was a hell of a lot of bats up there, but they did not come out by daylight, and the tinsmith returned, put in a new gutter, and the carpenter sealed up all the holes that he could find.

I took the children and went to Missouri, and Grant went to stay with friends. The fire chief was informed, a large warning poison sign was posted on the door (reported later by a neighbor child as "that skiliton on your house"), and the exterminators set the cyanide gas cans up inside the attic. For a week the house was uninhabitable. Thousands of bats were killed and had to be shoveled out by hand and lowered down the trapdoor in buckets. A few hundred escaped and went behind the shutters, from which the exterminator drove them with a mouse powder, and these died outside.

Well, it was done, and successfully, and gradually the incomparable smell of dead bats faded from the hot summer air; and we slept peacefully again at night without the soundless intrusion of little swooping wings.

But I was not wholly happy about it all, for bats on such a grand scale as ours seemed an extraordinary phenomenon, a hundred years' accumulation of life, and an act of God not to be tampered with too much. Would not

Nature take her revenge in some unknown and probably terrifying form? Sometimes at midnight I listened for the sound of monstrous insect wings, of mosquitoes hungry and humming in the dark, armed with the knowledge of their enemies' mass death, and come at last into their own. And beyond the sinister hum I heard the laughter of little bat ghosts, sneering in the night.

8 In May when the morning fog lifted it left the sea of bluegrass on the lawn covered with mist, the illusion of living in an aquatic world. The water dripped from the leaves onto this foam, and the sound of the birds was liquid. The delicate floating balls of the campion flowers with their white petals were suspended on such frail stems they seemed to swim like sea urchins in the watery air. Even the sky was still

white-silver with fog, and a few wet ghosts of the dandelion seeds hung dispiritedly on their hollow stems. Between the watery grass and the misty sky the birds moved like flying fish.

This damp silver interval was the hour of the snail. It moved its wet grayness along the vines more slowly than the vines themselves grew under its sliding stomach.

The snail, the *Illustrated Natural History of the Animal Kingdom* tells us, is a gastroped or bellywalker, and lays eggs the size of peas. "The reproduction of snails is most curious," writes Mr. S. G. Goodrich in the *History*.

> At a certain time of the year, they meet in pairs, and, stationing themselves an inch or two apart, they launch at each other several little darts, not quite half an inch long. These are of a horny substance and sharply pointed at one end. The animals, during the breeding season, are furnished with a reservoir of them, situated in the neck. After the discharge of the first dart, the wounded snail immediately retaliates on its aggressor by ejecting at it a similar one; the other renews the battle, and in turn is wounded. Thus are the darts of Cupid, metaphorical with all the rest of creation, completely realized in snails. After the combat they embrace each other and both lay eggs!

Mr. Goodrich also mentions the edible snail, which the Romans fattened with meal and wine in the cocklearia by the thousands, and whose shells were reputed to have held ten quarts—whether of wine or of snail he does not say.

The vines which climbed faster than the snails were Chinese yams, and their root stems supported a light-seeking head—a head which is a cross between an asparagus and a python, and moves with an eerie snake-like motion toward the windowpane. Alongside these vines grew the young elms and indestructible wiry, tough hornbeams, so close to this ancient house that their roots reached down into the cellar and their fresh arrogant branches tapped against the screens. They planned to reach the upper windows in time, and their roots went about a separate and seditious business underground.

Observing their tough will to live, it struck me, one day, that we might find the whole great house tipped up on end some morning, listing to port like a giant ship, and carelessly poised on the roots of the elms and the hornbeams—sun streaming into the cellar, gilding the cobwebs and the dusty mice.

Long before noon the water world had vanished. The sky was a dry white-blue. The green-and-silver grass was warm and polished by the wind. The ancient pine, higher than the house, fruited, bearing soft red cones that dangled like squirrel tails. These and the frosty green new growth gave it the strange festive look of a Christmas tree, trimmed in red and silver, heavily weighted, but calm and majestic in its unseasonable ornament.

The cats began to look motheaten and thinner in this month. They spent much time lying around sleeping and sprawled out on their shedding sides, feet over the edge of things. Nothing alert but a clump of whiskers. As one scrambled about, working, waiting, doing, listening, talking, the effrontery of these limp furry rags draped over tables and porch chairs, lying in the sun-and-shadow shifting of the maple leaves, began to work on one's harried soul. And so, although it was not quite clear what one had in mind the cats should *do*, since they cannot be continually on a dead run after mice, we thought of them with contempt, and of ourselves with pride because we had clumped back and forth around the house some twenty dozen times ourselves already and were exhausted by midmorning, and they had only raised one paw, and flopped it down again. And thus because of our envy we began to pass moral judgments upon them—the origin of many a moral judgment on the world—and found virtue in our inability to drape ourselves limply over a bench and feel the passing of the maple shadows back and forth across our faces, and listen to the far, faint sound of bees.

Were one to take the cat's-soul view of things, one might delight in all the gorgeous messiness of this May world. The flowering seeding bluegrass so thick there scarcely seems more room for its falling seed. Bird shells, sparrow nest, the willow blowing its cottony snowlike white dust-kittens, each tuft floating and following the air currents, finally resting in the grass, hardly distinguished from the white ghosts of the dandelions. And in this feline frame of reference one might see even the plantain, the bane of the tidy soul, as actually quite beautiful, and think of its silky leaves and ribs as of a water plant, a tropical hyacinth. "Ah," one might find oneself saying, "how well the plantain is doing this year, dear. Has it not truly repaid our tremendous lack of effort! And how lovely the lacy chickweed in between!" And "By George, I think we've nearly done for that bloody bluegrass after all this time!"

At six, the late May shadows were long and clear and moved across the soft blurry green of the lawn. The peony clumps were covered with enormous flowers, shaggy and spicy—some like the ruffs of white Chinese chows, or pink and blowzy, like overblown roses. The evening breeze lifted the warm aromatic scent from the soft hot flowers and sent it in waves across the lawn. The swallows began to swoop in the long low light. The great matriarchal house brooded quietly, its once great acres shrunken to this little skirt of three.

Later, the fireflies rose and sank on the uncut lawn. The children pursued the wandering lights and caught them as they rose upward, or pounced on the little lantern in the grass, Annie's hand sweeping softly downward like a kitten's paw, and then cupping the small cold light in both her palms. She was always fearful of hurting the firefly, and left too big a hole at the top of her hands, so that the dry tickling feet marched up their cage and the lightning bug zoomed away. A few bats glided and swooped in silence along the porch, under and over the trees. They streaked strange patterns between the house and the scattered stars. The fragrance of the peonies was cool and spicy now, without warmth. "Bedtime, children," the parent voices began to say. Brightly, hopefully. The voices had a calm honeyed sound which would not last, which cannot, and never has, and yet was part of that piteous parent hope—perhaps this time. Perchance, this time the ancient dream comes true whose roots lie God knows where—perhaps in the *Girl's Own Annual*, where, in dark engraving line, the nightgowned children mount the stairs and with clean sleepy faces place themselves between the sheets, murmuring, "Good night, Mother dear, good night, dear Papa. God bless you one and all, and thank you for this lovely day," and go to sleep.

But at last there was silence. A ghostly tree toad climbed quietly up the pane and pressed his little face against the glass. He devoured the white moths that fluttered their powdery wings in the light, and his little hands plucked out the inedible portions and cast them aside.

The weary people beyond the vision of his bright wet eyes sighed a little, stretched, and blinked their eyes. They would have liked to discuss deep matters with great brilliance, with insight and penetration probe the nature of Universal Truth, or with flashes of wit and wisdom light the history of mankind in its long journey through the spiritual night under the everlasting stars. But they were too tired from the journey itself.

The fireflies danced and the bats swooped and swung above the white mist, and the only sound was the faint murmuring of the night itself.

9 In a shoebox full of sand by the western window lived four lions. Probably the ugliest and most tedious pets a family ever chose to shelter. They had fat gray bodies and a big pair of falcate pincers on their heads, and the whole setup reminded me of the great Whipsnade Zoo which I once overheard two old gentlemen discussing on an English train as "the most frightfully boring place—the animals *never* come out, you know!"

Well, these creatures never came out, unless they came at night when no one could see them, and remained most of their lives, hidden except for their claws, in their little pits of sand, poised and tense, waiting for ants to come scurrying along, single-mindedly bent on business of their own, intent and unaware. The ant lion is the gray larva of a winged thing something like a dragonfly, spindle-shaped and small with mandibulo-suctorial-type jaws, with one small skill, the making of a pit in sand by backing downward, and one great gift, the ability to wait for days for food to come along.

But in their shoebox home no ants came naturally scurrying, to fall into the pit and be trapped by the sliding sand as they try to struggle upward; and even the lovely termite queens with juicy bodies and white luminous wings that suddenly materialized like ectoplasm from nowhere and glided over the living-room floor a few months ago were long gone about their dark and secret business under the earth, undermining the cellar beams. Food had to be artificially imported for the ant lions, and members of the family wandered about in the sun and rain, staring idly at their feet, not moody, thoughtful or halfwitted, but only hunting food for the myrmeleonidae.

This task was once much simpler when the route of an ant colony established in the roots of a maple tree crossed the concrete path of our sidewalk on their endless traveling to a willow tree where their aphis herd was pastured. Ants, black and large as ponies, galloped back and forth all day long, undeterred by storms that turned the walk into a Niagara and washed their bodies out to sea, and the willow leaves were full of herdsmen tending to their silent sticky little kine through all the daylight hours. Then suddenly, for some mysterious reason, they abandoned the route. The small dark beaten path under the grass was still there, worn smooth by countless chitined feet that hurried madly as most insects hurry. (What a relief to watch the mantis that moves with deadly dignity like a great sloth, or the still, armored immobility of the assassin bugs. Bees, ants, all the nervous zitzit things that fly and buzz and scurry, possessed of demon souls in the knowledge of the shortness of their lives—they can drive you crazy.)

The path was still there, but not an ant soul galloped over it. Perhaps reports of the great moonheaded hawks that suddenly swooped downward on the herdsmen eventually got back into the colony, or—a slightly more scientific explanation—they may merely have moved the herd to greener pastures for fear of overgrazing. Too many aphids, not enough honey. At all events, as the summer drew down to a close, ants seemed to get scarcer and scarcer, and the spring throngs that fought all over the kitchen and blackened or reddened the laundry floor like Pharaoh's army disappeared. It was high time for the lions to get busy on some metamorphosis into winged things or else curl up and go to sleep.

We had found the ant lions in a pile of sand back on the farm in Missouri, where they had written some obscure message on the sand in wandering hieroglyphics between the little pits, and brought them home when we went to get the children, who spent their summers where I spent most of my own childhood.

It is usually a mistake to go back to childhood places after a long absence. Time does curious and dreadful things to the well beloved, and one is saddened with real grief, or saddened by what is worse, one's own indifference and chill detachment to the change. Some spots at "home" in Missouri had not changed, however, other than to grow more as they were in the beginning; and the curve in the creek where my heart as a child literally stood still at the sight of a muddy muskrat slopping up the bank with a mouthful of grass was the same with its long stretches of rock and pools of captured water, the stream trickling through legions of purple waterweeds, whose name I once knew well, and the willow's tangles that advanced and retreated as the course of the creek changed with each storm.

We had all trooped down the hills in the morning heat, climbed the Never-Sag gate, and hunted for raccoon tracks in the brown gravelly mud. Annie had read a book on the preservation of tracks in paraffin, and so accordingly we carried with us a double-boiler bottom, still warm from the stove, with paraffin, rolls of cardboard for holding up the paraffin, and boxes for preserving the preserved tracks. The sun was hot on the flat muddy stones, a great melon vine escaped from the field in the bottomland wandered down to the water's edge under the willows with a few gold blossoms among its massive leaves. Annie waded into the brown water and followed the bank, some instinct telling her what a raccoon would do, and there on the creek's edge were the marks of little handlike paws that had come down to the crawfish shallows.

So like human hands are the paws that once when I discovered an old and graying raccoon dead by the roadside, the little outstretched hands seemed encased in the small black leather gloves, genteel and slightly striated, that old ladies used to wear, and I almost felt a pair of gold-rimmed glasses should be lying there, too, shattered on the road.

After the tracks were found it developed that the paraffin was too cool by now and so a small fire of leaves and twigs was painfully built in the mud and all the adult nature lovers gathered in a circle like sachems on the bank, with endless flowing advice on which was the best track, which the best way to fold cardboard and pour paraffin, and whether the sun was at the right angle of incidence.

Annie, with the beautiful calm and native deafness of the nine-year-old child, ignored this barrage of ancient sagacity and, lying to her waist in water, covered with mud like a muskrat, silently followed the step-by-step instructions in her how-to-do-it book, circled the track with a collar of cardboard, and poured the paraffin therein. The result a short time later was a beautiful clear print of raccoon paw with all five fingers and a lifelike little cushioned palm in the center.

The children had also organized a neat "insect-killing kit" from some magazine instructions and had so far chloroformed and impaled three ants and a fly. We went on an insect-hunting expedition to find more specimens for their collection, but it turned out that neither of the children wished to kill anything any more, and the Kit, being accomplished, was now regarded with considerable horror. And they refused to have anything to do with the death of a walkingstick, which Grant, with man's love of the laboratory tools, could not forbear to accomplish, since the Kit was all set up and arranged so neatly.

That was the month of the emerging locust, and the dry whirring sound, one of the most evocative of all sounds, wiping out thirty years in a second, creating again the sense of summer in childhood with an almost unbearable reality, came from all the trees in the late afternoon, and the little ghostly shells were scattered in the warm grass or clung brittle and brown to the bark where they had climbed. Quite often there is an odd regularity about their clinging, and when you find one ridged ghost a few feet up from the ground, directly above it will be another, and then a third above this one on the underside of a limb as though the same cicada had shed three shells in its long climb. For some reason children have never been afraid of these quaint and brittle things which are actually the exoskeletons of nymphs, and their empty honey-colored eyes hold no terrors; and so instead of snuffing out more insects, Annie gathered the innumerable pale shells until her basket held almost a pint of little ghosts, and a pint is the limit of a connoisseur; after that one might as well rake leaves and call his pile a "collection."

We found the pale-gray toadstools with fluted silk and the stairstep fungus that grows on trees, first soft and ominously white, and then turning brown and green and barklike and taking on the shape and color of a grouse's tail. The acorns had started to fall and were green and satiny with a peachlike fuzz. Some were still joined, with their green cheeks pressed together, just as they had plummeted from the rejecting twig above. Left alone they would dry and shrink and roll away from each other on the blind business of getting born, leaving their small scalloped platters still joined like the abandoned hats of children.

In August one year came an incident which took place not on the farm in Missouri, nor on our insect-stocked three acres in Ohio, but in an ice-cube-sized apartment in New York, where, in the heart of the city, my sister Marjorie raised a window garden of such magnitude that she claims not even Gene Stratton Porter had such favorable "conditions" for nature watching. Among pots of horehound, lilies of the valley, alyssum, sweet basil, mint, lace vines, bracken fern, sage and coriander, not to mention sweet peas, marjoram, plantain lilies, ruta, and thyme, she grew a plot of parsley. And thence came the phenomenon of which she wrote—the changing of a swallowtail worm into a chrysalis, that little living tomb in which it spends its time before emerging as a butterfly.

I am compelled to write you of an incident, which in its small way was as terrifying as any I have ever experienced. Of how—after twenty years of Nature Watching in more appropriate places—on a window sill, where sound is drowned by the roar of buses, I was at last accorded the fearful privilege of Intimacy with Creation; and the thing is this:

Some weeks ago we were distressed to find the small patch of parsley in the garden was being absolutely denuded by parsley worms—the beautiful green-and-black-striped one you no doubt remember. First a black stripe, then pale green, then a black stripe dotted with yellow . . . The kind of worm which can be translated by illustrations of German gnome and fairy stories into a cheerful habitant of magnified leaves and flowers, or by the puppet maker into a jolly clown, easily identified by bright splashes of stripes, and the object of admiration for its ingenious construction. (Usually a spring, covered with an enviable bit of velvet.)

. . . It was difficult to do away with four such jeweled creatures and so we housed them in a glass jar and bought them a handsome bunch of parsley. (A bunch much too large for ordinary household use was only twelve cents.) For several days they ate, devouring not only the leaf but the stem, until their delicate jaws sensed things were getting too tough and it was time to travel.

Then one day, although a new bouquet was bought, the water changed, the emerald fecula carefully removed, they became restless and hurried around the jar looking for something that evidently was not there. We responded with twigs (is it not wonderful that they will accept nothing that will wilt or break or freeze?) and after they had each fastened themselves by three silken threads they hung all day on the twigs absolutely quiet, their color only slightly changed, their bodies only slightly shrunken.

At five-thirty in the evening the last worm to anchor himself to the twig began to move again, weaving his head back and forth, and we wondered if he had changed his mind, or was not yet ready for the little death. And whether, as sometimes with one who has taken an overdose of sleeping pills, he could yet be roused and made to walk again. At five forty-five I happened to look again, and what I saw has really shaken me for two days.

Stretching, pulsing, his face had dissolved! The weird face of the worm had become a fibrous, flat green mask of a cat, the two horns protruding upright like pointed ears. A mass of tiny knobs had burst from the shoulder area. The feet had gone entirely, leaving only a smooth green in the front, though the body was still marked in rings.

The whole object stretched, expanded, shrank again, as though it were a body which could feel the pain of corruption after death, or a Pharaoh, strong-willed enough to pump his soul through the tiny ventricles of linen and spice. The wings, wet with a solution of dissolved matter, lengthened and thickened, changing from a ring-marked mass to a smooth wing shape, as though to be prepared for instant flight with the expected verdict on judgment day.

By six-thirty the movements became slower and slower, only a little pulling, a little stretching. The outer case became smoother, the wing shapes folded close to the body, a swelling appeared in the abdomen—and then all movement ceased, the little thing dropped closer to the stem, lying against its binding threads, to shrink and wait.

It was, perhaps, a fitting finish to those creatures who alternately fascinated and terrified me. But I shall not feel safe until Osiris calls them up, past the brief humiliation that even a god must suffer as he passes through too small a door, to the light where only the bars on their lovely wings will remind them of their other selves.

10 Hot damp days came in June at the Old Place. The rugs curled damply like wool salamanders. Outside the sun was bright and hot. The lilies, white madonna lilies, a glaring white. The mulberries ripened—as ripe as the birds would permit. There is a moment when they are not ripe even to a bird, and the bird sits there patiently and impales them with his eye until his burning gaze brings the sugar to a boil and then he beaks them, and no human has a chance.

One day after torrential rains came a beautiful pure afternoon. The washed light flowed over the cornfields. The corn was about a foot high, and what appeared clumps of round white stones scattered all over the field were giant mushrooms or puffballs. They looked incredibly edible. Each one big enough to smother a steak alone. Six inches across and their tops like a wrinkled soufflé. A delicate fawn brown, which against the fields' wet chocolate seemed blazing white. The air felt clean, blowing over the earth and the corn and the doeskin mushrooms.

The summer evenings were flooded with the smell of honeysuckle and roses and madonna lilies. Two-year-old Carol smelled delicious when she was a little hot and sweaty, and divine when she was clean. She spread her little fat starfish hands over her mouth as children do, and ate food off her palms. She had delicate plump motions. Scratched the curls at the nape of her neck, blew at cotton balls or feathers. Touched noses with all resemblances to living things—pictures of cats, plush Easter chickens. But no child ever thinks it is "cute." Only the observer. Children are serious little old people inside all the time. But to me she seemed enveloped in a great bubble of purity. A priceless and unbreakable enclosure.

> *Ko ni aku to*
> *Mosu hito niwa*
> *Hana mo nashi,*

wrote the poet Basho—"There are no cherry flowers for

those men who say they are tired of their children. Why, a child is a flower, so to speak!"

At the eastern corner of our ancient house was an old woodpile. Under the beautiful shadow of the wild cherry trees and maple it had lain for years and was now overgrown with grapevines and honeysuckle, sheltering chipmunks and itinerant skunks that wandered through on summer nights. In the small space of those logs and crumbling timber, an infinite, minute world went on, almost soundless, often invisible, but continuous, shifting, full of faint scents and changing lights. By early autumn the grape and honeysuckle were covered by the weightless sprawling vines of the wild cucumber, whose lacelike spires of flowers had changed to prickly clusters of fruit, and whose twisting hands, delicate as watch springs, had grabbed onto every perpendicular stalk they could wrap themselves about. Their mindless loving spirals circled the Queen Anne's lace, and the handles of the broken wheelbarrow carried their luminous green fruit, which dangled like spiny hedgehogs under the wide umbrella leaves.

The various bees of the world, from the great mumbling giants to the small brown velvet bees like winged moles, moved over the cucumber vines, which flowered and fruited at the same time. In the early mornings these cucumber leaves were stiff and spread out in the dew like lily pads, but as the sun moved slowly over the woodpile they collapsed weakly into soft mushy rags, and the path of the sun was marked by their fainting shapes. But no matter how closely I watched I could not detect that mystic moment when the cluster of cucumber pods, silver and sticky as a bunch of burs, became *one* cucumber. Was *it* chosen to grow of all the lot, and did the rest reluctantly drop away—Oh, never mind us, it doesn't matter, we'll just wither up here in the grass while you grow big and strong—or did one secretly *devour* all the rest, spines and all, on some moonlit night and emerge The One next morning?

By the summer's end the woodpile was a mass of bindweed vines with their small white flowers, of morning glories whose delicate seedpods are shaped like winged buds, and the enormous grape leaves were insect-riddled, some shadowy as lace. In the dark cool recesses under the logs grew the shelf fungus, velvety and soft, and the swollen body of a brown earth cricket moved along the shelves, preoccupied and withdrawn in its pregnancy, waiting for the signal of its time. Sleek as a chestnut, it stepped sullenly around the small white cups of the bird-nest fungus, some filled with minute egg spores waiting for a bird not larger than a bee, and some empty and white as porcelain.

The English ivy that grew in a mat outward from the house and never climbed, seeming unable to attach itself to the painted brick, crept each year nearer to the wild vines of the woodpile; and, watching a wasp pick its elegant nervous path along the sliding and shining leaves, one realized suddenly the *moving* floor that insects tread, the delicately articulated shifting floor of leaves. The ivy bends and trembles under the wasps' feet while we clump heavily over the solid floor of earth.

While pondering on this one time I saw a small

black spider asleep above a leaf, his head bowed on his arms (or feet) like a sleeping cat, when suddenly the small black toady head jerked up and I looked directly into the creature's eyes. What an overwhelming experience! Those glittering darts of jet seemed the essence of unwinking evil. Refined and crystal evil of such purity that it held you frozen to the heart. For a long and horrid moment we stared at each other, and then it disappeared among the ivy leaves. As I thawed slowly back to normal it occurred to me that the encounter might have made some impression the other way around. What did *it* think of *me* in that chilling moment? "My God," was he saying to his wife or some fellow arachnid, "those great empty evil pools of green! Cold as autumn algae. I *saw myself* swimming in them! How shall I ever forget this?" And they would have huddled together like two black hairy toads, thinking of what incredible situations one encounters in this world.

We had a small vegetable garden at the Old House. The rich plot of ground that our neighbor hopefully plowed each year with his tractor started out rich and chocolate brown each year, and stakes were set up to give a professional and tidy air. Then came the selection of vegetables, which was remarkably limited, since the children liked only beans and carrots and cucumbers, and the rest of us could not eat Brussels sprouts or cauliflower or cabbage. Potatoes, which our predecessors grew by the bushel, would yield for us nothing but strange little plants like old Christmas trees stripped of needles and bright and heavy with bright beetle balls.

So we planted only a few rows of beans and cucumbers and a row of corn.

Then up through the glistening chocolate soil all around these rows came the native crop of cockle and wild amaranth, dock and sorrel, and the bindweed— which, given time, would cover all the world including the various oceans, and the earth would hurtle through space a globe of green clinging vines like a monstrous ivy ball. This was always a source of considerable shame and sorrow to us through each summer, but one autumn, wandering through our seedy jungle, I thought, with that stubborn core of brightness which is innate in gloomy souls—I thought, No, by heaven, the fruits of neglect are many and wonderful, and the harvest, although *different* from other people's, has a richness all its own. It was not that we would not have preferred the golden and substantial harvest of more industrious men, the cellar, the freezer, the flowing bin—but, faced with the wages of sloth, the devious soul inclines to polish up this tarnished coin, and use it in those realms where it has a value all its own. This harvest of ours was a tide of morning-glory vines, whose leaves had turned to a gold and dying brown, and some of a polished eggplant color, and in the tide floated blossoms of pure and delicate purple and magenta.

Also there were green branches of the wormwood weed, delicate and lacelike, branched like cedar trees, with an indescribable aromatic autumn scent, like fir and spice and marigold. The wild green-and-red amaranth, though an ugly and furry weed, has a long history, both as food for ancient people and as the center of religious rites. We gathered a few stalks and beat out the glittering black seeds that looked like birdshot and were each smaller than a pinhead. Grant resorted to various devices to rid the seeds of chaff, blowing on it in the manner of the ancient gleaners, until he looked like an engraving of the West Wind driving ships at sea, and then used the water treatment by which all—or most— of the bright-eyed seeds fell to the bottom and the chaff floated. This last worked fairly well, and when they were toweled and dry we got out a frying pan and dumped them in.

In the meantime the children had decided this was the day to dig up the ant lions and change them to another home. They passed them about for us to inspect their louse-shaped bodies and scimitar horns, and held out the lions with one hand while they shook the seeds in the frying pan with the other, and talked about their "popping well." The bright black seeds of amaranth did begin popping soon, but though we tried two batches, one delicately fried in oil, we could not keep them from scorching and they tasted about as delicious as burnt sand. They may well require that added touch of human blood, but the general feeling was to give the amaranth back to the Aztecs where it came from.

In the tangle of the manifold weeds, the praying mantis, a valuable insect and more effective against the devils than red amaranth, came each year and built —exuded—its spongy nest. One of the strangest sights is the laying of a mantis' eggs. They are "layed," nest and all, in one curious foamy operation, as though the mantis had become a green tube of shaving cream, and out of her abdomen foams the gold froth which gradually hardens in the air like a brittle sponge, and clings to the vines or weed stems through the winter, holding the eggs, from which will step briskly minute mantises in the spring.

I found one enormous female suspended among the buckwheat vines, her thin thorny arms in the ominous posture, not of prayer, but of anticipation; and near her a furry brown-gold caterpillar came crawling along the vines. It came nearer and nearer, and she watched with her pale terrible eyes its nibbling progress around a leaf. Then the caterpillar came to the end of its leaf and reached out blindly to eat on, its jaws grazing the mantis on her leg. In that moment it became suddenly and terribly aware of the pinpoint eyes in their gray orbs watching above it, and retreated, humping, hurrying, actually rippling with horror, at the nearness of its death.

The mantis was probably already satiated, and about to bear her nest, because later when I brought her a new grasshopper, stump-winged still, with only gray lumps where its wings should have been, and unable to do anything but crawl, she regarded it coldly and did not stir, seeming to be preoccupied inwardly with the spongy delivery which was to come.

All around us the land was flat for a mile or so, gashed and white with the gravel quarries, and underlain with ancient limestone and acres of glacial stones.

There were old and new quarries, and some of the old had filled into small lakes, blue and pure as only a quarry lake can be.

And some of the gashes and holes had become small ponds and arroyos, with a willow-rooted, algae-blurred life of their own. Toward the end of summer these willow ditches dried down to a mere leaf-filled dampness, and along the final margin the algae clung to the hairy willow roots and dried, white and weblike, making rows of fishermen's nets all up and down the length of the vanished pool.

In the fragrant shadow of the dying willows, in the bed of ancient black willow leaves from other years, there is a minute world of little dry dead things, fragile and of myriad shapes—tiny shells like ram's horns, pure white among the black leaves, and the hollow halves of microscopic burs, prickly and brown as porcupines. The transparent wing of a cicada is there, and the white *ghost* of a dragonfly. Under the circled cottonwood leaves, whose dry cupped paws are not gray, not brown, but sepia, the color of old faded photographs, were the larger whorled shells of snails abandoned to the winter, and once I found the delicate backbone of a bird.

September ended with a long dry wind that seemed to have blown without stopping from some Western desert. For several days it blew, full of dust scents and the dryness of sage brush, and went on blowing eastward, carrying our own autumn smells of falling maple leaves, green walnut and the warm lemon odor of quince and yellow apple. With such long and level blowing all scents must have reached the Atlantic and there mingled with foam and cooling sands, the smell of salt and fish and marshes. And then at last, lost in the sound and smell of breaking water, the scents and fragrance sifted downward on the beaches, under the same autumn moon that saw them starting eastward on their journey.

11 At the Old House the first frost came on the sixth of October. In the morning everything was silver and icy, the tall grasses delicate as glass and blue with a frosty bloom. The earth was sheathed in frost; and after the sun rose, the shadows of the house and trees were blue on the ground, and all around them, defining them, the sun-released grasses turned wet and green. The hard maple at the end of the

144

road had turned gold in every leaf and stood motionless under the morning moon, which looked naked and lost in the blue sky. A solitary crow flew over between the moon and the lighted tree.

The early part of October was a beautiful and uncertain time, cold and wet and dry and warm. The trees had a drying yellow color all over the countryside, with only a solitary burning light here and there. Our black kittens moved out with distaste carefully into the cold mornings. One was a new imported Persian kitten, who seemed out of place among the vines and falling leaves and autumn disorder. He was a few months old when we got him and had never been out of a house, but was so big already—so enormous, in fact—that we named him Monstro, and he padded about like a furry whale. He regarded each descending leaf with terror, and spent his first days glued to the door. As time passed he ventured into the long grass step by step, sniffing the menancing weeds and shying away from grasshoppers. He watched the other kitten, Minx—who was only a quarter Persian and had an odd wild face like a pine marten —catch a vole, and sat respectfully two feet away, a kind of furry wonder on his big child face. After a while he caught a grasshopper for himself and even went alone as far as the woodpile and the edge of the giant grasses in the garden.

We had bought him as a companion and future mate for Minx, the last of Fuzzy's children, who had the long thin body of her mother and the same sweeping tail, but not the wise Egyptian head or the ancient wisdom. Fuzzy died in August a slow sad death, of such incredible dignity it was like watching an old queen go down slowly into darkness, and even I, who have none of the vast sentiment that seems to flow from most of the world toward the cat kingdom, cried for a long time and can still be dissolved by the memory of that wasted classic head full of twelve years of matriarchal burdens and feral independence, sinking down on the helpless paws.

Monstro had quite a place to fill, but his tremendous warm purr, like a giant bee in his throat, and his affectionate clasp around one's neck, appealed to the children, and he was quite a sight, moving big and black among the gold leaves, with his innocent gold eyes, enormous and inquiring.

The chickadees and the field sparrows came to the ruined amaranth garden, and the asparagus ferns turned to a saffron mist, in which a few solitary berries hung like red balls and the white asters were caught and swam starlike in the dry mist.

The great mantises, having laid their nests, disappeared, and only a few gray smaller ones were left here and there, mantis-shaped bits of bark, with the same cold balls of eyes and the long scaly arms. On hot days the autumn crop of butterflies came out, and I found a violet-tip, newly sprung, almost outrageously colored in new orange, with a purple aura around its flaming velvet wings. Hundreds of yellow and saffron cabbage butterflies floated above the asters, which gave off a faint honey scent of autumn.

As the month drew to a close, the pond life sank into sleep, the trees emptied in the wind, but the incessant, jerky, nervous life of the insects diminished reluctantly. On a warm day, if you opened an unscreened window, in the mistaken idea that since it was October and winter was coming one might as well get all one could out of the season, the room was suddenly streaked with long-legged and still unsleeping wasps, with wandering humming bees, and the bullet flight of the great bottle fly.

The Chinese yams, the cinnamon vines, which covered the windows on the west side all summer, were thick with little tubers that looked like fairy potatoes, and the leaves shriveled from a deep gold to curled brown. The "potatoes" look startlingly like Idahos and are about three quarters of an inch in length. They showered from the vines at a touch, and, having heard that they were edible, we decided to give them a go—although they would have been more appropriate perhaps to the hidden bins of small people Annie and I imagined inhabit the roots of the willow tree. Annie gathered a pan of the tubers, which bounced like dry peas, and carefully, with her small fingers around a knife which seemed giant, pared off the skin and dropped the almost invisible remains into a frying pan with butter. Some we saved without paring and boiled in their jackets. The little potatoes tasted like big potatoes, and with salt and butter struck the children as something rare and special and very edible for costing nothing. (Since then we have learned that there are hundreds of wild vegetables like that, but the potatoes were first.) We followed them with a few things someone else had raised by hoe and plow—big slices of fried eggplant, and polished green peppers, enormous yams, dry and sweet with brown sugar, and a salad of yellow pear tomatoes, luminous and shaped like little flasks—and nobody's appetite seemed much diminished by the first course of wild starch.

The far, strange origins of Halloween, when the ghosts of Celts came whimpering in from the frosty pastures and the empty Irish woods, to warm their wasted hands by the peat-bog fires and the warmth of their living kin, are lost now in the welter of dime-store witches and soapy windows. The ritual and the legend are become prank and established custom, as does anything that lasts beyond the wonder of religion and of awe. And life being more precarious, death more widespread, less uncertain, we no longer build the Coel Coeth bonfires as in ancient Wales, and cast the life- or death-predicting stones, for omen of who lives or dies, before the wheeling year brings back All Hallows' Day again.

The dual heart within us both rejoices and regrets the passing of this terror and this awe. Or perhaps it is only because we are too old to bob for apples and beg for candy, that we think of Halloween now as cardboard pumpkins in the first-grade windows, of crayon witches all alike, and children in their costumes. Since *we* are no longer rosy-faced among the rosy apples, nor smitten to the heart by gypsy bangles, nor terrorized by painted skeletons, we seek our awe in conjuration of another century, when the legend was both real and new, and forget that we could re-create that child to whom the platitude held terror and delight because she herself was new.

Some night late in autumn came one of those seasonless hours of darkness and warmth when, in the October moonlight, leaves beat suddenly against the kitchen pane, and a great flowing wind poured through the barren maple branches. And with it there seemed to come a revelation of enormous freedom out there in the darkness where the witches begin to ride, and the bodiless souls go rushing down the wind. Grease grows suddenly cold and gray in the dishpan, and the baby cries out with pure meanness. Visions of years and years of anxieties unresolved, of waking nights, of measles and heartbreak and decisions, of the responsibility upon us to protest, and the responsibility to conform, the burden of example and of kindness—and suddenly would come a knowledge of that freedom we have never known, the weightless, boundless disembodied freedom of the soul who has bartered flesh and blood, and made his night pact with the smiling Satan. . . . It would seem very near and close, this hour of the flying leaves, this promise and this revelation.

By the end of October, though all else was drying and the woodpile vine shriveled and brown and the white fungus hard, the maple reached its peak of gold perfection. Every leaf was a clashing, moving jewel, leaves of beaten gold, and it shone through the dark pine trees like an army of angels coming down in rays of light. For a day, if there was no wind, it stood there, a great gold burning bush, absolutely still, awesome in the shape of beauty beyond which there is no further shaping, and then the wind would rise. That which was before only the movement of a bird was the falling of a leaf. Then another leaf, and then a shower of leaves. In a few hours the gold was thinner, the emptying tree no longer a burning cloud, the shape of the branches becoming clearer and clearer under the descending shower. By morning it was all over and the maple tree stood gray and anonymous, like the framework of a fountain, winter-stilled, above the great yellow pool of its own leaves.

12 We had ten years of spring and summer and autumn in the Old House. Ten years of the gold maple. Ten years of winter. The house was beautiful in all its hours. Sunlight streamed through the eastern windows, made those long gold-mote paths we tried to climb as children. Sunlight streamed from Grant. We thought things were as they appeared to be. We had a past and a present and a future—all five of us. It was the high noon and the summer of our lives. Of all our five lives together.

But there was too much house, too little land. There were times when I was so tired I wondered if the other end of the room would be ever reached, and the spider webs on the ceiling seemed up among the stars. Then the quarries grew and the valley was mined and undermined, pocked and pitted, down to the graves of Indians and the last mammoth bone. We loved our great drafty matriarch, but loved land and living things and greenness and silence more. Like Grandfather Franklin we conceived our own plan of moving to the country, and so in a way we *left* our Oakland, our mansion of many rooms, and moved into another world.

One time I looked back, looked down into that once beautiful, now ruined, valley, and it was as though the intervening years had all been washed away, and I saw the mammoths moving through the morning mist, the great arcs of their tusks that ran with rain. I saw a valley full of snow that was once a sea and then a plain. The mammoths came through the falling snow. Their long brown hair crusted with snow. The sound of their trumpeting hushed in the snow. They broke through the frozen crust and trampled the snow into giant hollows. The hairy domes of their skulls rose above the small cold eyes. . . . All gone now. Centuries gone. The land is covered with scars and gravel pits, concrete highways and graves of the elms and sycamores. The lights are out in the caves and campfires. Dust and smog cover the valley plain.

But the Old House was the most beautiful, the most

memorable, of all the shelters, all the homes, on the long journey.

Hillbrook house. Gray stone house built by Father on farm outside of Kirkwood, Missouri.

Opposite, Josephine, twenty, writing at desk under dormer window. Hillbrook house.

Grant Cannon. "Grant came from Utah, from a valley surrounded by deserts and mountains; where one lived in the presence of mountains and the presence of pioneer ancestors from the hour of birth."

Annie and Terry in April at the Old House

The Old House, our first home, Newtown, Ohio. A homestead with a history that went back more than a hundred and thirty years.